Voyagers

Voyagers

Words and Images
Herb Kawainui Kane

Design
Robert B. Goodman and
Herb Kawainui Kane

Text Editor
Paul Berry

Managing Editors
Robert B. Goodman and
Lorie Rapkin

Published by WhaleSong, Incorporated
A Beyond Words Publishing Company Special Edition

First Edition
September 4th, 1991

Published by WhaleSong, Incorporated
12505 Bell Red Road, Suite 208
Bellevue, Washington 98005
(808) 595-3118 · AppleLink: WhaleSong

Library of Congress Catalogue Card Number 91-66341
ISBN 0-9627095-1-4
"VOYAGERS" was entirely created in PageMaker on the Macintosh color desktop with a Barneyscan 4520 scanner, and an Agfa SelectSet 5000 imagesetter.
Typefaces used in this book are Goudy Village No. 2 and Goudy Sans from The Font Company, Scottsdale, AZ.
Printed on 80 pound S. D. Warren Cameo Dull by Dynagraphics Printing Company, Portland Oregon.

The artist may be contacted directly by writing to:
P.O. Box 163, Captain Cook, Hawai'i, 96704.

Words

Kapingamarangi
Samoan Islands
Tahiti (Society Islands)
Manahiki
Marquesas Islands
Caroline Islands
New Zealand
Tuamotu Islands
Tahiti

IMAGES:

Editorial advice, corrections, and reprimands by Alexandra Halsey and Frank Miller.

This book brings together less than half of the paintings and sculpture completed over the past two decades, and very few of the drawings. Regarding all my art works with a certain parental affection, I found that the selection could not be made without agonies of indecision; and to those collectors who may not find their works among these pages, I can only say that to omit them hurt me all the more.

Some of the paintings are a storyteller's interpretations of myths and legends. Others are carefully researched reconstructions of moments in history. But many others are of no history but my own.

HULA HOLOKU

The dancer wears a *holoku*—a formal 19th century dress with a long train—and traditionally dances barefooted. The painting suggests the flowing, graceful movement of the dance by superimposing several images of the dancer as she moves from side to side and slowly forward.

Early missionaries promoted the wearing of the *mu'umu'u*, a loose sack-like dress. The more formal holoku was worn on special occasions. It is still a tradition; annual *holoku* balls are held with prizes for the most outstanding designs.

Collection of Terry Russ

HINTS ON
HAWAIIAN PRONOUNCIATION:

a as in ah
i as ee in see
o as in so
e as ay in day, or as e in men
u as oo in too

Pronounce every syllable.
Pronounce each vowel separately:
Laa is Lah-ah
The hamza or glottal stop(') indicates that at one time a consonant appeared in that place but has since been dropped.

Herb Kawainui Kane

Publisher's Preface

STORYTELLING AND TECHNOLOGY are as old as man. Whether we choose to stone-chisel petroglyphs into volcanic rock or click on a computer icon to produce an entire book, we are driven by the common need to tell our story.

The early Polynesians created chants to preserve their geneologies. They navigated their double hulled sailing canoes across thousands of miles of open ocean, guided by the paths of stars, by the waves and swells. Both their storytelling and their technology evolved as expressions of harmony with the natural world. As we approach the close of the 20th Century we are faced with the challenge to restore that balance.

More than 25 years ago, I had the good fortune to meet Herb Kawainui Kane. Storyteller, craftsman, sailor, navigator, historian, popular anthropologist, naval architect and artist, he is truly a renaissance man of the Pacific. In *Voyagers*, Herb has harnessed the power—*technology infused with inspiration*—to pull the history of his people out of the very air in which they walked, up from the seas they sailed. For me, there is something about a Herb Kane painting that draws me in, in toward those tiny details, something that prompts a voice inside to say, "I want to *look* at this!" Herb's words and images invest the record of his people with the power of dream and myth. *Voyagers* is a remarkable gift to us all.

Not surprisingly, this book contains a story within a story. Like so many other voyagers, I came to Hawaii years ago looking for that balance of technology and inspiration I call "high tech - soft touch." I've found it in a Nuuanu hillside home where, today, Lorie and I pursue our publishing path, exploring the new worlds opened up by the Macintosh desktop revolution. Surrounded by trees, we have created a laboratory for electronic color prepress, from scanning to typesetting to page layout to imagesetting to proofing.

Voyagers, as a demonstration of our new storytelling technology, is part of the history playing out across its pages. It is the first full color art book ever to present both text and images created entirely on the desktop (see page 162). Like the impact of Captain James Cook's arrival in these islands, the arrival of new electronic publishing tools has changed the landscape of individual expression forever.

I invite you now to turn a page, to become part of our story, and let us become part of yours.

Robert B. Goodman
Honolulu, Hawaii

THE PETROGLYPH MAKER
Along the ancient trail that passes 'Anaeho'omalu (now Waikoloa Beach Resort) on Hawai'i Island, thousands of petroglyphs tell of those who stopped to record their passage over the centuries.

Much speculation has been offered, but little is really known about the meanings of these rock carvings. Some may have been clan emblems; others may have commemorated events. They are treasured today as evidence of the original culture of Hawai'i, irreplaceable and priceless.

Collection of Elizabeth Marshall, M.D.

BANYAN AT HONOLULU ZOO *Collection of Bharat B. Behan*

BEING THE ONLY BAREFOOT BOY in a noisy crowd of well-dressed grownups no longer bothered me once I had seen the paintings. I was stunned, confronted with miracles.

The occasion was the 1935 opening of an exhibit of the art of Howard Hitchcock in Hilo on the Island of Hawai'i. And there, in the center of the uproar, stood the magician. While my mother chatted with friends, I took refuge in quiet corners from which I could safely view the paintings.

Sometime later I was startled to see the artist approaching, his eye on me. I could not move. He said a few pleasant words, but all I could remember was that he had actually spoken to me. I went home and began crayonizing every scrap of paper that came to hand.

Although my father played the guitar and ukulele well enough to sell lessons, when he got around to teaching his two sons, he learned that it was my brother who had the talent for music. My musical inadequacies were vastly amplified when I joined the school band and brought home a trumpet, blowing on it as if I were Joshua shattering the walls of Jericho. All I succeeded in shattering was my father's equanimity. Observing that Hawaii had an abundance of musicians but few artists, he decided that there might be some relief for himself—and a future for me—if he encouraged my drawing habit.

HI'ILAWE
Neighbors gather for songs and storytelling in this scene remembered from the artist's childhood in Waipi'o Valley. In the background is Hi'ilawe Falls in the moonlight.
State Foundation Collection

LEARNING

From an early age my father's gifts as a storyteller infected me with his love of legends and history. Friends of a similar mind would come by in the evening, and I would fall asleep listening to the tales being woven out on the veranda. On our visits to the family home in Waipi'o Valley, where the past has an almost tangible presence, such nocturnal talk around the kerosene lamp would eventually turn to folk tales and ghost stories, each progressively more fabulous and frightening. Later, when a call from nature demanded a response, it became a test of courage to get up, part the mosquito net, and sneak out into the dreadful darkness.

In high school, storytelling through painting became my great interest. I was inspired by the work of American regionalists Thomas Hart Benton and Grant Wood. After serving in the Navy, I enrolled at the Art Institute of Chicago, but discovered that representational art which conveyed a mood or message was no longer labeled as real 'Art,' but as 'mere illustration.'

With the death of regionalism, art faced the new requirement of being 'universal.' Craving acceptance from my peers, like any twenty year old, I applied myself to learning formulas for what then passed as advanced theories of painting; that year it was abstract expressionism.

Every profession must have its area of experiment as well as its area of application. But while I viewed the 'new wave' painting experiments as interesting basic research, they were, for me, slender fare. The subtle and diverse challenges of realism held far more fascination.

Of all possible art subjects, *Homo Sapiens* has always held the most interest for *Homo Sapiens*. Artists who represent the human figure with skill and sensitivity will find larger and more

HAWAIIAN REVERIE *Collection of Joseph and Katherine Drew*

THE MERMAID OF WAILEA
Left: The mermaid Wewehe, a younger sister of Pele, lived at the shore at Wailea, Maui. A friend of sea mammals, she enjoyed swimming with whales as they passed by on their annual migrations.
Limited edition bronze

LEAVING LAHAINA ROADS
Right: Thrashing into the tradewinds with a bone in her teeth, a trading schooner of the early 1800s sails out of the lee of West Maui. A cargo-carrying double canoe is heading the other way. Such ships became the backbone of inter-island commerce during the early years of the Monarchy.
Collection of "Buzz" and Kimberly Pauley

interested audiences than artists who do not. There have been great painters of landscape, still life, and natural history subjects to be sure, and in this century some outstanding painters of non-representational art; but the history of art is largely the family album of humanity. Ironically, of all subjects, it is the human figure, the one subject with which viewers are most familiar and critical, that proves the most difficult. Learning to draw this figure with authority has allowed competent figure painters to surmount this difficulty, but then competent figure painters have always been a minority.

That minority is smaller today than it has been for centuries. Learning to draw, which is learning to see clearly, requires a laborious effort in which there is no instant gratification. Drawing classes have always been unpopular with art students, which may be why they are no longer required by art schools or university art departments, where the primary concern seems to be keeping up enrollments. The assumption is that drawing is not fundamental to current art theory. As a consequence, the more than 35,000 graduates now spawned annually have, as artists in the real world, about as much chance of survival as baby salmon.

It was my good fortune to attend art school at a time when learning to draw was still believed to be fundamental. In our compulsory drawing classes a few unreconstructed old-timers on the faculty, by virtue of their own astonishing skills, served as drawing masters and teachers of figure painting. Under their tyranny a student might be led through the basic skills, then his eyes opened to such enchanting nuances as color and tonal relationships, design, the sensitive treatment of edges, uniformity of surface, spatial relationships, mood-producing use of light and shadow—all the old stuff that got washed out by the new wave. Even at the cost of the good opinion of my peers, this was what really interested

KAMAMALU

HONOLULU FISHMARKET *Collection of Allen C. Wilcox, Jr.*

me. I decided to become a 'mere illustrator.'

Having vowed to earn a living by his art, a professional artist must keep the brush moving if he is to develop, and he must find a market if he is to survive. In the past such markets lay in the need of religions to glorify their teachings, the need of ruling classes to promote their status, and the desire of those successful in trade to enjoy their wealth. Today the need of private enterprise to innovate and advertise dominates the market for an artist's skills.

To the consternation of my parents and in-laws, I turned down two respectable teaching jobs, put my master's degree in the closet, and found a job as an apprentice in a busy commercial art studio. The partners optimistically invested a salary of $60 per week hoping that I might someday develop a level of expertise that would bring some work into the studio and give them a return. I should have been paying them.

Here, alive and well, was the ancient master-apprentice system, only superficially different from the way it had operated since the Middle Ages. Then students were taken into a studio, taught how to grind colors, make inks, prepare canvas, draw, and paint, all as quickly as possible so that they could be of some use. They would imitate the master, and eventually he might let them work on the less difficult areas of his paintings. After some disagreement an apprentice might get kicked out, and find another master, thus broadening his experience. It would not be a bad thing if this happened several times, for after successively imitating a number of masters, he might create a synthesis in his own work; his style would mature and become distinctive as his own. In time he would become sufficiently competent to paint his masterpiece, and if this solo work were approved, he could enter the guild as a master himself. This system of learning art by observation, demonstration, and practice has proven most effective, for art cannot be learned by lecture or book.

My masters were well-respected illustrators and graphic designers. I did production art (preparing graphics for photo-reproduction and printing) to make myself useful. I practiced illustration on my own time; and after my 'samples' began to show some competence, I was handed those cheaper jobs which did not interest the highly paid illustrators. There were opportunities to get their criticism, to observe them at work, and to absorb their discipline and professionalism. After several years I moved on to another studio which offered better assignments. Two years later I formed a studio with another artist and a salesman, and after another two years, tiring of advertising work, I disbanded the studio and began freelancing.

Advertising art paid well, but it was not the kind of storytelling I wanted to do. I could not look back on having created anything of lasting value. The end came when I won a Green Giant campaign, and for a year did drawings and paintings of that big green fairy until I could no longer suffer it. My agent threw a fit when I told him it was all over, but it was time to move on to something else.

Story illustration for magazine and book publishers paid less but was much more fun.

CAMAKAU OF FIJI
Throughout Polynesia the traditional sailing canoes have been replaced by boats with outboard engines; but the single-hulled outrigger *camakau* (pronounced "thamakau") still exists in the Lau Islands of Fiji. During the fuel shortage of 1973 these vessels served for subsistence fishing and transportation.
Private Collection

A fascination with history led to assignments to create illustrations for historical stories. At the same time, requests from architects for renderings led me to explore architectural design.

HOW THE CANOE BROUGHT ME HOME

After I had spent too many years in Chicago, my father admitted that my survival as an artist had not been as improbable as he had feared. He suggested that if I now wanted to make any worthwhile contribution beyond raising his grandchildren, I should consider returning to Hawai'i. The idea began to take root, and visits to the islands became more frequent.

I had been attracted to Chicago by the School of the Art Institute and the University of Chicago, and I was held there by the city's vigor and the professional opportunities which both the Chicago and New York marketplaces offered. But I knew I could never belong there.

A United Airlines jet may have transported me to Hawai'i, but it was really the sailing canoe that brought me home. I had sailed on Hawaiian fishing canoes in the days before outboard engines. In Chicago, heedless of mentors whose advice to young illustrators included the avoidance of such diversions as alcohol, loose women, and sailboats, I bought a catamaran as soon as I could afford it. Time which might have been better devoted to artistic self-development was spent beating about that treacherous inland sea, Lake Michigan. (notes: 1)

My interests in art, architecture, Polynesian traditions, and sailing found a common focus in the Polynesian voyaging canoe.

A *WA'A KAULUA* OF HAWAI'I

Above: Sailing was the primary power mode for the ancient voyaging canoes, the distances being too great to travel by paddling. The classical Hawaiian canoe evolved later as a design more suited for paddling. Dangerous political waters made it prudent to take numerous bodyguards on inter-island voyages—men who could also serve as paddlers, enabling chiefs to travel in any direction without waiting for favorable winds.

The arched crossbeams connecting the hulls are uniquely Hawaiian, attributed to the 17th century designer Kanuha.

This painting conforms to measurements recorded by the Cook expedition of a canoe of the King of Hawai'i, Kalaniopu'u: length 70', overall beam 12', hull depth 3' 5".

Collection: Hawai'i State Foundation on Culture and the Arts

WAR CANOES OF THE NEW ZEALAND MAORI

Right: Brandishing his jade warclub, a champion issues a challenge as his double-hulled sailing canoe closes on a single-hulled war canoe of another clan.

Collection: Hawai'i State Foundation on Culture and the Arts

THE SHARK STRIKES AT SUNDOWN
Rising to the scent of a basket of rotten meat, a shark is lured into a weighted noose slung between the hulls of a double canoe. In the painting the line is payed out as the shark continues moving forward. A moment later the line will be jerked taut and the canoe will be taken on a wild ride. After the shark tires, another noose can be slipped over its tail, and the fish pulled backward until it drowns. The belief that sharks feed closer to the surface when the sun is lower in the sky cautions many Pacific Islanders against taking a sunset swim.
Artist's Collection

Early Europeans in the Pacific had made sketches of canoes, most of them ineptly rendered and tantalizingly incomplete. Inaccuracies, obvious to any sailor, piqued my curiosity.

I set out to uncover everything I could about the actual dimensions and seaworthiness of the canoes, beginning with the most comprehensive work on the subject, *Canoes of Oceania* (notes: 2). I gathered additional photographs and measurements of Polynesian canoes and canoe fragments in museum collections, and searched for other bits of information on canoes and voyaging that were not found in published works. With help from anthropologists Terence Barrow and Kenneth Emory in Honolulu, doors now opened to collections and archives worldwide. Assembling the bits of information made it possible to reconstruct some of the canoes in architectural drawings. Then I did paintings based on the architectural drawings, depictions of how these vessels must have appeared when manned and under sail on the open sea.

I was hooked. Despite having a family to feed and a bank balance that looked more appalling each month, I found myself turning down good assignments to pursue my obsession with the canoes of Polynesia.

Fortunately friends in Hawai'i came to the rescue. Dillingham Corporation purchased the right to reproduce the paintings in their 1972 and 1973 promotional tide calendars. At Kenneth Emory's suggestion, Robert Van Dorpe introduced the fourteen paintings to the State Foundation on Culture and the Arts. Chairman "Pundy" Yokouchi brought the matter to the board, and Director Alfred Preis purchased the lot. Lieutenant Governor George Ariyoshi hosted an exhibit at the State Capitol. Robert Goodman offered to publish a portfolio of prints of the work, and introduced me to *National Geographic* Editor Bill Garrett, who commissioned a series of seven paintings and an illustrated map insert about Polynesian voyaging traditions that was published in December, 1974. Graphic designers Tom Lee and Momi Cazimero offered me studio space. At Bob Van Dorpe's suggestion, John Kay offered me a design consultancy on C. Brewer, Ltd. resort projects. The canoes of another time had brought me back to Hawai'i.

A *TONGIAKI* OF TONGA

The *Va'a Tele* of Samoa mirrored the same design of the *tongiaki*. In 1619 the first contact between Europeans and Polynesians at sea occurred when the Dutch explorer Schouten met a *tongiaki*. He wrote:

"The rig of these vessels is so excellent and they go so well under sail that there are few ships in Holland that could overhaul them."

When the Cook expedition arrived at Tonga, these vessels were being replaced with the double-ended *kalia*, similar to the Fijian *ndrua*.

Collection: Hawai'i State Foundation on Culture and the Arts

NDRUA OF THE FIJI ISLANDS

Right: The Fijian *ndrua* (double canoe) was known in Tonga as the *kalia*, and in Samoa as the *'alia*. Developed in the 17th or 18th centuries, these were the swiftest sailing vessels of Polynesia. Double-ended, these canoes were tacked by reversing the positions of the sail, spars, and steering sweeps from one end of the canoe to the other.

"It had a magnificent appearance with its immense sail of white mats; its velocity was almost inconceivable." (Wilkes, 1840).

"Up went the huge sail, down went the great steering oars, splashing into the sea, and away we shot like a racehorse. Owing to the great rate at which we were going, the sea was like a hissing cauldron on either side of our course, and the vessel, instead of having time to mount over the smaller waves, cut its way through them." (West, 1869).

A *ndrua* named *Rusi i vanua* (cursed is the land) was measured at 118 feet in length. Its deck was 50 feet by 24 feet, length of mast 68 feet, and length of yards 90 feet. A steering oar in the Suva Museum is 33 feet long.

Collection: Hawai'i State Foundation on Culture and the Arts

TORCH FISHING FOR FLYING FISH AT ATIU, COOK ISLANDS
Above: On still nights the *malolo* are netted as they surface or leap toward torchlight. Nocturnal fishing parties were occasions for much humorous banter as each man took his turn at the net. The technique is still practiced in Tahiti, using outboard-powered skiffs and electric lights.
Collection: Hawai'i State Foundation on Culture and the Arts

A VA'A MOTU OF TAHITI
Right: Swift sailing outrigger canoes of this design were used throughout the Society (Tahitian) Islands.
Collection of Ron Becker

A *TIPAIRUA* OF TAHITI

Tipairua carried such romantic names as *Wait for the West Wind*, and *Rainbow*. Their sails were a local evolution from the triangular oceanic sail. Sir Joseph Banks (1769) wrote:

"With these sails their canoes go at a very good rate, and lie very near the wind, probably on account of their being bordered with wood."

Collection: Hawai'i State Foundation on Culture and the Arts

A WAR *PAHI* OR CEREMONIAL *VA'A TI'I* OF TAHITI

Right: In 1774 Captain Cook witnessed 160 of these vessels accompanied by 170 smaller double-hulled sailing canoes carrying *"not less than 7,760 men"* to battle. Used for ceremonial purposes as well as war, such vessels took years to build. Hulls were of carved breadfruit planks built up over dugout keelpieces and assembled with sennit lashings.

Collection: Hawai'i State Foundation on Culture and the Arts

A WAKA TOU'UA OF THE MARQUESAS ISLANDS

Left: Bird symbolism is seen the the profile of this canoe. Lacking abundant lagoons and plagued by periods of drought, the Marquesas spawned many voyages in search of new lands. Hawai'i and Easter Island may have been first discovered by voyagers from the Marquesas. One account of a voyage of exile was heard in the early 19th century by Captain David Porter of the U. S. Navy:

"The grandfather of Gattanewa sailed with four large canoes in search of land, taking with him a large stock of provisions and water, together with a quantity of hogs, poultry, and young plants. He was accompanied by several families, and has never been heard of since he sailed."

Collection: Hawai'i State Foundation on Culture and the Arts

AN ANCIENT VOYAGING CANOE OF THE ERA OF EASTERN POLYNESIAN EXPLORATION

Right: For this reconstruction the 'age-distribution' method was used, assuming that canoe design features which were most widely distributed must have been features of the original culture. This painting includes sail and hull design features found throughout Hawai'i, New Zealand, and the Marquesas at the time of European contact, and in a petroglyph of an Easter Island double canoe.

This painting was the basis for the design of the voyaging canoe replica *Hokule'a*, which differs only by the inclusion of distinctively Hawaiian features that do not affect performance.

Collection: Hawai'i State Foundation on Culture and the Arts

HOKULE'A I
Left: This 60' replica of an ancient voyaging canoe made round trips between Hawaii and Tahiti in 1976 and 1980, and a 16,000 mile pan-Polynesia campaign (1985-1987) visiting islands between Hawai'i and New Zealand. Its voyages have been navigated entirely without instruments.
Collection of Ann Bentley Jorgenson

HOKULE'A II
Right: The canoe has been welcomed everywhere as a symbol of mutuality among all Polynesians, truly the "spaceship of our ancestors." It's now based in Honolulu, and still sailing.
Collection of Everett and Ellen Mayhood

HOKULE'A

There was no one alive who could answer the questions. For long years scholars had argued whether Polynesian navigators had the ability and the vessels to master the vast Pacific. I knew now how the old canoes had been built. What if we actually built a full size replica of a canoe incorporating the functional design features most widely distributed throughout Polynesia? Putting such a canoe to an actual test would test as well the accounts of Polynesian navigation. An actual sailing could provide data that might settle this long dispute. Even more intriguing to me was the thought that recreating the central object of the ancient culture and taking it to sea might stimulate the growing interest in a cultural revival. (notes: 3)

The idea attracted others. We incorporated as the Polynesian Voyaging Society and recruited members. I drew a preliminary plan for such a canoe, then made a painting. Feeling altogether foolish, I found myself flashing the painting around Honolulu, asking for money. Hundreds of volunteers came forward to contribute time, talent, and substance, and the canoe got built.

We launched it in 1975. When others looked to me with the question: "You got us into this. Now how do we sail this sixty foot vessel with weird-looking sails and no rudder?" Using what I had learned from sailing catamarans, I found myself as the training skipper. It was not easy. On shakedown cruises throughout the Hawaiian islands, we were literally relearning the past.

CANOE RACE *Pentagram Corporation Collection*

TWO FISHERMEN
Right: A net thrower on the Kona Coast—and a petroglyph of a fisherman in the foreground.
Collection of Colin and Mary Love

It was a wonderfully satisfying experience, but not without nerve-wracking moments. Sailing with green hands in an unforgiving vessel was a constant reminder of my old mentor's admonition about sailboats.

Navigated without charts or instruments, this replica of an ancient Eastern Polynesian voyaging canoe made two 5,500 mile round trips between Hawai'i and Tahiti in 1976 and 1980. Another very successful voyage in 1985-87 took it from Hawai'i to Tahiti, Mo'orea, Huahine, Ra'iatea, the Cook Islands, New Zealand, Tonga, Samoa, then back to Hawai'i by way of the Cook Islands and Tahiti—a round trip of 16,000 miles between the northern and southern points of the Polynesian triangle.

We named the canoe *Hokule'a* (star of gladness), the Hawaiian name for Arcturus, a star which appears to pass directly overhead on the latitude of Hawai'i, and was thereby useful as a navigation star for the ancient voyagers. At every port of call *Hokule'a* was warmly received by Polynesians as the symbol of their mutuality, and a reminder of the resourcefulness, inventiveness, and courage of their ancestors. (notes: 4)

Presently berthed at the Hawai'i Maritime Center, the canoe continues to be sailed by the Polynesian Voyaging Society.

I was once interviewed by an advisory committee to the Hawaii State Foundation on Culture and Arts on my application to do a work of sculpture for the University of Hawai'i. Most of the committee members were on the University faculty, including a sociologist who posed a formidable question that went something like this:

"Mr. Kane, could you produce a sculpture

ON THE LANAI *Collection of Leo and Lee Chamberlain*

SUNDAY AFTERNOON *Collection of Michael and Valerie Warren*

that would be a comprehensive interpretation of the entire society of Ancient Hawai'i; one that would express the world view of those people, their premises about the natural universe, their level of technology, their science, their craftsmanship, their sense of space and time, their values, their aspirations, something of their social structure ..." As he droned on, a glance around the table showed Executive Director Alfred Preis beginning to slump. Others were gazing out of the window. I searched my mind unsuccessfully for a polite response. Struck by a sudden thought, I replied:

"Sorry, but that's already been done."

"It has? Where is it?" someone asked. Everyone was now fully attentive.

"At pier 12 in Honolulu Harbor. It's a piece of functional sculpture, actually a mobile, and it is truly interpretive of everything you've asked for. It's title is *Hokule'a*."

There were a few grins around the table, but I sensed that my reply was generally taken as a smart-aleck remark.

I did not hear from the committee again.

ESCAPE FROM URBANIZATION

After the 1976 voyage was successfully concluded and all debts paid, I moved to the district of Kona on Hawai'i Island. Although Honolulu is still my favorite city, it was becoming too much a suburb of Los Angeles.

When I was a boy, my father occasionally took us on trips to Kona, on the leeward side of Hawai'i Island. Kona is shielded from the trade winds by three mountains. Its climate, and the polite social climate of its people, made it a tranquil place.

In Kailua, the largest village, a dog could lie down for a nap in the middle of the main road, and cars and horses would not disturb it. Kailua was then, as Mark Twain had described it earlier, "*the sleepiest, quietest, Sundayest looking place you can imagine. ...Ye weary ones that are sick of the labor and care and bewildering turmoil of the great world, go to Kailua! A week there ought to cure the saddest of you all.*"

By 1985, however, the urbanization of Hawai'i had caught up with me. The Kailua I had known had disappeared, along with it my peace of mind. North Kona was now regarded by frenetic real estate developers and salesmen as their private casino, and players were coming from the Mainland and Japan in ever increasing numbers. Too many newcomers were bringing along as mental baggage the turmoil they were trying to leave behind.

It was time to move again, this time to rural South Kona, where what little remained of Old Hawai'i was still hanging on by its fingernails. Given the civility and warmth of its people, South Kona is one of the most endearing places in the world. (notes 5)

THE LITTLE MERMAID
One evening, walking along the shoreline of South Kona, my attention was focussed down on my footing over the uneven lava. When I had last looked up there was nobody to be seen, so I assumed that I was alone.

Glancing up I was startled to see a little child, silent and still, watching me from a tidal pool. No one else was in sight. She seemed to have appeared as if by magic.

The spell was broken moments later when I heard voices above the sound of the sea. Moving on, I saw men in the water diving for sea urchins, and two women on shore scooping the roe into buckets.

The image of the silent child remained with me. Years later I put it down on canvas.

Collection of Deon Satterfield Kane

At this point, my time was divided between painting and consulting on the design of resort projects in Hawai'i and Tahiti, and cultural centers in Fiji and Hawai'i. In 1980 I abandoned design work to concentrate on painting. Once again, that which rewarded me psychically cost me financially.

There's a handicap in being a living artist. Artists face competition not only from contemporaries, but from the work of dead artists as well. Once an artist is good and dead, and all his works have been cataloged and evaluated, investors have a much greater sense of assurance in buying. The critics and dealers will make pronouncements upon the significance and price structure of his work. If his work has made a favorable impact, he has, by the act of dying, done a great favor for all who own it. In the tension between supply/demand, supply is now fixed. Moreover, the artist can no longer do anything stupid that would have an adverse impact on demand—such as changing his style so that critics might say he has lost his talent. (notes: 6)

Short of having a stroke, artists rarely lose their talent, but many have learned that a change of style can be sudden death. The fall of De Chirico's popularity when he abandoned the surrealism for which he had been 'typed' offers but one example. Only a few artists as shrewd and playful as Picasso have successfully orchestrated changes of style to the delight rather than the discomfort of their publics.

Art collectors who have a good eye toward

PA'U RIDERS OF OLD HAWAI'I (II)
Above: Disdaining the "side-saddle" position, Hawaiian women preferred long, full riding skirts (*pa'u*) which enabled them to straddle their horses. They would often spur their mounts to full gallop to make a dramatic arrival at a party.

The tradition of wearing the pa'u is kept alive today at parades and celebrations throughout Hawai'i.
Collection of The Chart House, Inc.

KAHALU'U SUNSET
Right: The locale is Kahalu'u Bay, Kona, Hawai'i.
Collection of Sonny Iwamoto

investment and a willingness to gamble on the work of a living artist want to feel fairly certain that the artist will produce a "significant body of work" in his lifetime and not be just a "one-hit Harry." The overall impression made by everything the artist has done will affect the resale value of each piece.

That is why—as my savings evaporated—most collectors viewed my full commitment to painting from a wait-and-see position. Fortunately, several did not. The willingness of Nick G. Maggos and Jay Rose to add my work to their collections now made a significant difference.

And when other collectors began to step forward, I had turned the corner.

KAHUNA KALAI KI'I
A priest-carver of temple images.
Collection: Hawai'i State Foundation on Culture and the Arts

KA'ANAPALI 200 YEARS AGO
Right page: Once a Maui fishing and farming community, now the site of a popular resort.
Collection of Amfac/JMB Hawai'i

DAYDREAM *Collection of Nick G. Maggos*

PAINTING AS TIME TRAVEL

If an artist cannot get excited about his work, no one else will. A painting or sculpture is a statement, a tangible expression of an idea. The artist's enthusiasm in the performance may affect forever the attitudes of viewers. An artist may have talent and training, but if he has nothing interesting to say, or is intimidated by critics, or is overly concerned about what happened to be "hot" in New York last week, then neither he nor his work will long survive.

For an unabashed storyteller, ideas for paintings are not a problem. In the history of Hawai'i and the South Pacific I have found a rich source of imagery, sufficient to provide ideas, work, and excitement to fill several lifetimes.

Historians of scholarly mien have informed me that history is a science, implying that artists would be well advised to stay out of their tower. But history has no value to society if its findings are not communicated,and many historians have difficulty communicating, except among themselves. Writing in private jargon, scientific historians may succeed in putting lay readers to sleep in their first paragraphs. But the great historical writers, knowing that the historian's task clearly includes both a high quality of research and the art of communication, have regarded telling the story of history as an art. Although this is conventionally done with words, I believe that painting has the power to create a sense of history beyond words.

There are in the U.S. only a handful of artist-historians, painters who cultivate the discipline of the historian but whose end products are pictures rather than words. Each of us has our areas of special interest, having progressed from being a "buff" about a subject to becoming a "nut", which is the term some of our spouses prefer over the more charitable "authority."

Like most folks, I must earn a living, something I prefer to do by the sale of my art. As a bonus, some collectors have become good friends. But there is more. If my work contributes to our comprehension of Hawaii's past, that will ultimately become the greatest reward.

After viewing one of my paintings of Pu'ukohola, the war temple of Kamehameha, depicted as it may have appeared two centuries ago, a young Hawaiian admitted that he had always regarded the present remains of the old temple platforms as "just piles of rock."

"But," he continued," you show me not only the rock platform that remains today, but the buildings, the altar, the fire—all gone now. And you even show the people. Even if they restored the place, they could not bring back the people.

KAUILA

In a time of storms a great sea turtle laid an egg in the black sand beach at Punalu'u, Ka'u, Hawai'i. Scooping up sand to cover it, she created a large freshwater pond behind the beach.

The egg hatched into a little turtle. The people named her Kauila because her shell was the color of dark brown kauila wood. A mermaid, she could turn herself into a little girl and come ashore to play with the children. When sleepy, she would turn into a turtle and retreat into the pond for a nap.

As she grew, she could take the form of a beautiful maiden, but when young men made advances, she would turn into a turtle and escape into the dark pond.

As you walk along the pond today, you can see air bubbles rising, a sign that she's still asleep.

This folktale became the subject of a painting, and later a sculpture. Built of rigid polyurethane foam with a modelling of polyester resin over fiberglass, the sculpture floats. Water trickles from the seaweed head *lei* and keeps the piece glistening as if the girl and the turtle have just risen from beneath the surface.

The Painting: Collection of the Punalu'u Black Sand Beach Restaurant
The Sculpture: Artist's Collection

THE PINK PAREU *Artist's Collection*

After what this painting said to me, I can never again look at any *heiau* as just a pile of rock."

I treasure that compliment far beyond the price I received for the painting, for it helps me believe that my work will outlive me with a life—and voice—of its own.

If I have been particularly attentive to the time between Captain Cook's arrival in 1778 and the end of Kamehameha's reign in 1819, it is because the events of those years were pivotal, shaping Hawai'i's subsequent history far out of proportion to the importance given to them in their time. Also, from some of the most casual and sketchy records of that period we may glean precious insights into the original culture and people of Hawai'i. In those years the Tanata Maori—as Hawaiians then knew themselves—awakened to the outside world and to the bewildering crossroads of demands, choices, and dangers from which they could not turn back. It was a time of desperate struggle to survive epidemics of foreign diseases, a time to adapt to new ways and create a nation that would gain recognition by others as sovereign unto itself. It was a time in the context of the Chinese curse: "May your sons live in interesting times."

Chinese painters observe a saying: "To paint a flower, you must be a flower; to paint a tiger, you must be a tiger," which is to say that an artist must empathize with his subject. Depicting a people of another time and culture requires such empathy. Without it, the figures cannot come alive on the canvas; they either appear curiously wooden or as depictions of the artist's models—modern persons in period costume.

TERNS AT TETIAROA *Collection of Mr. and Mrs. Ralph S. Hemer*

A FISHING CANOE OFF NORTH KONA *Collection of William and Diana Holland*

This lack of empathy is one reason why many Hollywood films about people in other times are so unconvincing.

Where the subjects are people of a primal culture, the difficulty of empathy is a major obstacle. Primal cultures are essentially much alike, as proved by the universality of their myths; but world views, beliefs and attitudes of primal societies are so fundamentally different from those of the modern western society that what may be perfectly logical to one group may seem bizarre and incomprehensible to the other. The artist can bridge this chasm of differences only insofar as he can bring himself to see the world of his subjects through their eyes. (notes: 7)

Such empathy cannot be achieved by those enchanted by romantic or sentimental sympathy. Historians who succumb to emotional partisanship can never gain a clear view of their subjects. All peoples indulge in romantic nostalgia; the making of myths and moral judgments about the past is a universally popular pastime. Such myths may reveal fundamental truths about those who made them, but they can also blind us to the truths of history. As the historian peels away the accretions of romantic fancy that obscure the past, he may well be rewarded with the nuggets of truth that lie beneath.

The Invisible Artist

ithin a few seconds after going on stage, a skilled actor can disappear, transforming himself into the character of his role. His own personality becomes invisible. This is not self-expression. It is interpretation based on the actor's ability to discover the essential personality of the subject. Similarly, a painter can empathize with his subject only by opening himself to it, striving to keep his own personality out of the way, and allowing the subject to speak to him about how it should be painted.

Such invisibility comes from looking outward rather than inward. The popular theory, however, is that art must be the unfettered expression of the inner creative self. Self-expression through art has become the theme of children's art programs and psychological therapy. Art students, too, are led to believe that only through agonies of introspection can they find themselves, develop their own unique, personal style, and drink of the dark wine of genius. Taken seriously, this stance means that the artist himself inevitably becomes the subject of the painting. Indeed, a young man who recently graduated from the University of Hawai'i with a master's degree in painting informed me that he does not exhibit his work because he feels it is "too personal."

A unique and distinctive style, that nagging worry of many artists today, is best achieved by simply not fretting about it; for just as everyone's handwriting is unique, every artist will lay down his brushstrokes in a unique way. If the painter has achieved empathy with his subject, style will take care of itself.

Observing that my work is representational and not reflective of current art theory, the same young painter asked if I was concerned that my work was not "timely."

I confessed that being timely doesn't interest me. Fads and fashions rise and fall in art like the hemlines of skirts. Much to the dismay of investor-collectors, some painting mannerisms that seemed so ravishingly new in one decade have a way of looking embarrassingly quaint in the next. My interest lies in producing work that I hope will prove not "timely" but "timeless."

Representational art is a tradition as old as the superb drawings of animals on the walls of Cro-Magnon caves. Since then artists have recorded, commemorated, celebrated, and critiqued their peoples and places. It is a tradition certain to survive those who would discard it today.

Of No History But My Own

If you thumb through this book, you will notice that not all the paintings are heavy efforts at historical depiction. Hawaiian composers have always taken license to write songs about whatever caught their fancy—be it the flashing eyes of a pretty girl, the beauties of certain places, the cascading of a waterfall, the pitching and rolling of a little inter-island ship, or the rhythmic prancing of sandpipers along the edge of the sea. Many of my paintings follow that same tradition, having nothing to do with any history but my own. Glimpses of places and people, some from faraway childhood, moments that express something essential about the Hawai'i I've known and love; these have a way of staying with me, until out of necessity, I put them down on canvas.

DAUGHTERS OF THE SEA

Left: A time remembered when a *mu'umu'u* was the only acceptable bathing attire for Hawaiian women. The painting expresses the artist's childhood memory of young ladies floating gracefully upon a gentle sea, their long garments billowing in the clear water.

Collection of Patrick W. Hopper

NIGHT FISHING IN OLD HAWAI'I

Right: As the sky darkened, men prowled the shallow waters of lagoons with torches and spears. Candles used for lighting homes were made by stringing dried nutmeats of the oily kukui nut on thin bamboo skewers. As each nut burned, it ignited the nut below it. Clusters of these candles were carried in a hollow bamboo to make a torch. Spears were hardwood shafts six to seven feet long, the tips tapered to a point and fire-hardened.

Collection of Lewis and Dara Strauss

PAINTINGS FROM THE BOOK
VOYAGE, The Discovery of Hawai'i

Herb Kawainui Kane (*Island Heritage, Ltd.*, 1976)

This book, now out of print, was written as a seaman's tale of how the first voyage of discovery to Hawai'i may have taken place. It is illustrated by fifty paintings and drawings. The story is followed by notes on canoes, navigation, and other aspects of Polynesian voyaging that could not be gracefully included in the narrative.

The story begins on a drought-stricken island in the South Pacific with a battle between two communities over dwindling food resources.

The battle is lost, the champions slain, the ruling chief wounded. The victorious enemy agrees to an armistice on the condition that the defeated chief, with his family and a number of retainers, depart on a voyage of exile.

Excerpts from the narrative:

Where were we to go? We were too few to conquer another valley on our island, or any of the islands nearby. We were orphans of this land, and must find another.

During the time his wound was mending our chief's sleep was troubled by a strange dream. While his body slept, his

THE BATTLE *Collection of Roger Hendrickson*

FLIGHT'S END *Collection of Douglas L. MacArthur*

spirit arose and wandered down to the beach. Looking northward, he saw a tiny bird flying towards him from far across the water, flying low over the waves and struggling to stay in the air. Fluttering over the surf, it fell to the sand.

And when our chief's spirit picked it up and stroked its feathers, it turned its eye toward him and said,

"The path of my flight is your bearing. Sail!'

Thus it was decided. Each year we had seen these shore-birds flocking together and heading out over the horizon which led to the unexplored northern sea. There must be land to the north, for we knew these birds could not rest on water.

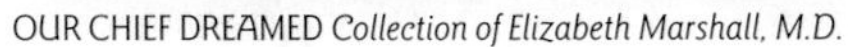

OUR CHIEF DREAMED *Collection of Elizabeth Marshall, M.D.*

THE MESSAGE *Collection of Samuel Ka'ai*

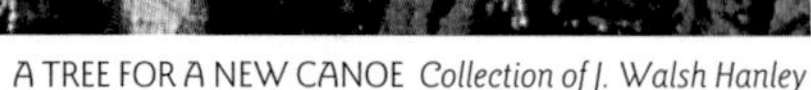
A TREE FOR A NEW CANOE *Collection of J. Walsh Hanley*

PREPARING SEA RATIONS

The chief's three double canoes are readied for the voyage with new sails and lashings. The narrator tells how he had helped cut logs for canoe hulls:

In the mountains we cut the logs from sacred groves, the stillness of the forest broken only by the sound of our adzes.

Canoes were regarded as living beings:

When a giant of the forest trembled and began to fall, the priest-craftsman shouted: 'Today you are a tree. Tomorrow you will become a man!'

Dried provisions and well-oiled water gourds were assembled. Seeds and young plants wrapped to protect them from seawater. Our best implements were packed. Young pigs, chickens, and dogs were selected. All that was necessary to sustain life on a long voyage and make possible the beginnings of a new settlement must be carried on the canoes.

Old men braided coconut-husk fiber rope for the lashings of the canoes. Women plaited strips of pandanus leaves into strong matting for new sails.

From among the commoners the chief selects those who will accompany his family as crewmen for the three canoes. When all is ready, the voyage begins.

BRAIDING SENNIT

PLAITING SAIL MATTING

SOME MUST BE LEFT BEHIND *Collection of Han Wilking*

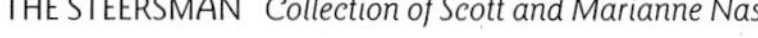

THE STEERSMAN *Collection of Scott and Marianne Nash*

WE ARE IN ANOTHER SEA *Collection of Phillip Hooton*

LOOKING AT THE NEW STAR

As they sail north, they are becalmed in the equatorial doldrums. The navigator, by the taste and temperature of the water, senses that the canoe has entered a new current, and announces:

"We are in another sea."

On the seventeenth night the breeze freshened, variable at first, then hardening from the east. By dawn, plumes of spray were bursting from our bows as our ships plunged northward with increasing speed.

In the South Pacific the North Star cannot be seen—north is a dark area of sky over which stars arch on their nightly paths. One night the navigator discovers a new star just above the horizon in the center of the place of darkness. A north star!

And as time passed the new star did not appear to move! Shaken by the importance of his discovery, the navigator called to the steersman. Soon everyone was awake to see this miracle, this star that did not move. We watched it throughout the night and could not cease speaking of it. Could it have been placed by the gods to light our way to new land?

IN THE NORTHERN SEA

THEN WE SAW THE BIRD *Collection of Michael and Cathy Clifford*

Of the three canoes, one disappears in a storm. Now the prevailing wind and seas are shifting to the northeast, heading the canoes.

The sea was running strong, raised by the velocity of the wind, and we knew that the lashings could not long endure the pounding of such waves. Lured by the new north star but unable to sail toward it, we were forced to accept a course to the northwest. In these winds the foresails alone were adequate to drive the ships.

On the twenty-sixth day we ate the last of our food, a few mouthfuls of dried fish and scraps of dried breadfuit paste. Our animals could no longer stand.Our water had been replenished in heavy rains, but now that was almost gone.

The women—how brave they were. Weak from starvation and exposure, they huddled together quietly. My wife, I can remember the moment so clearly, looked at me through salt-encrusted eyelids and warmed me with her smile

There had been no sign of land in all this northern sea; no drifting branches, no birds, no hovering clouds reflecting the green of sunlit lagoons, no sign of life except for a herd of great whales crossing our wake. How would it end?

On the afternoon of the next day a massive cloud bank on the western horizon appeared to be standing still, not moving in the wind— a sign that it might be building over an unseen island. Should we run down to it?

Then we saw the bird. It was homeward bound after its day of fishing. Flying low over the water, it headed straight for the strange cloud bank in the west, and we knew land was near. We put the wind astern and followed it. Porpoises appeared and frolicked alongside the canoes as they hurried westward. Had they been sent to guide us?

The Belittling of the Menehune

Mythical Hawaiian leprechauns
—or Hawai'i's first people?

SK ANY TOUR conductor: the Menehune were a race of little people, some say two feet tall, not unlike the gnomes, leprechauns, or elves of ancient Europe. Working in great numbers, these strong little folk could perform such feats as the construction of great voyaging canoes, huge temple platforms, long irrigation watercourses, or large fishponds. Each project was done within a single night or left unfinished. If they didn't want you to see them, the Menehune could become invisible.

On Kauai you may see solid evidence—the rockwork lining an ancient aqueduct, the "Menehune ditch," that once brought water from the Waimea river to irrigate dry lands for growing taro. The rocks were shaped and fitted together—a method of stonework requiring immense labor, and not typical of Hawaiian rockwork. At Nawiliwili the large Alekoko fishpond is said to have been built by Menehune. In the building of temples such as Malae Heiau at Wailua, it is said that Menehune passed rocks from hand to hand in long lines that stretched across the island.

If they liked you, they could be helpful. One story (which has other versions) holds that a boy named Laka needed a sailing canoe for a voyage to a distant island in order to rescue his mother from enslavement by a demon chief. He found the Menehune in the high forest and made a deal. Although they were mountain dwellers, they relished seafood. They agreed to build the canoe for him if he would give them a feast. While he netted fish and prepared the meal, they built a great canoe and carried it down to the seashore before dawn.

Modern storytellers have embellished the old stories and invented quite a few of their own. Bookstores and tourist shops throughout Hawai'i feature childrens' storybooks about cute little "Menehune" and their magic.

Another story, however, reveals who the Menehune really were—full-sized Polynesians, and the first discoverers and settlers of Hawaii.

Hawaiians measured their history not in years but in generations. By counting the generations in the chronology of the chiefs, anthropologists formerly placed the discovery of Hawai'i at around 900 years ago. Legends speak of canoes arriving from the leeward Tahitian islands of Ra'iatea and Bora Bora.

That assumption was shattered when archaeologists found Polynesian materials dating much earlier. More recent finds have pushed the settlement of Hawai'i back to about 1,900 years ago, possibly earlier. Similar finds elsewhere mark this as an early era of widespread exploration

Looking anew at the clouds we saw a sight difficult to comprehend. What had appeared as an unusual cloud formation was now revealed as the peak of a gigantic mountain, a mountain of unbelievable size, a white mountain— a pillar that seemed to support the dome of the sky! We watched in wonder until nightfall. Then to the south of that mountain a dull red glow lighted the underside of the lifting clouds, revealing the shape of another mountain. It brightened as the night darkened. That mountain seemed to be burning!

No one slept that night. Our two ships thrashed along in the night wind, and the dreadful red beacon lighted our way.

THE DISCOVERY OF HAWAI'I
This painting was not done for the book Voyage, but as part of the development of the Jaggar Museum, Hawai'i Volcanoes National Park, wherein a photomural is displayed.
Collection: Hawaii State Foundation on Culture & the Arts

THE STORY OF LAKA

Laka's parents sailed away on a voyage, leaving the boy with his grandmother. Years later, migrating birds stopped by to tell her that the demon chief of a distant island had killed Laka's father and enslaved his mother.

Laka vowed to build a canoe and seek vengeance. In the high forest he cut down a great tree. The work took an entire day, after which he went home to sleep. Returning to his work in the morning, he was surprised to see the tree standing without an adze mark on it. Again he cut it, and again on the following day there was no trace of his work. He felled it again, but this time he hid in its branches. That night little forest spirits gathered to raise the tree. Laka leaped from hiding and caught their chief.

When the spirits heard of his need for a canoe, they decided to help him. They built a great canoe in a single night, and carried it down to the beach.

Laka sailed with seven companions. In a distant sea he was attacked by monsters guarding the island of the demon chief. Laka and his men slew them all, including a gigantic squid and a great shark. Landing on the island, he killed the demon in a bitter struggle and rescued his mother.

The story is told with variations throughout Polynesia.

Collection of McDonald's of Hawaii

originating from the Marquesas or Tahiti, spreading as far as Hawai'i, Easter Island, and New Zealand, the most distant outposts of Eastern Polynesia.

The chiefs with whom the Hawaiian traditions originated are now regarded as late-comers who conquered those already here and erased their history.(notes: 8) These "Tahitians" came from Ra'iatea, Bora Bora, and Huahine, a cluster of islands where cultural change and new religious ideas had brought great status to the ruling families. Their "vatican" appears to have been the great temple Taputapuatea on the island of Ra'iatea. Their superior status was confirmed with genealogical proof—direct descent from the senior gods, a connection by which godly power *(mana)* could flow most directly and exclusively to them. No others need apply.

History shows us that such notions of superiority can become highly dangerous to others, which in this case meant all other Polynesians. *Manahune* was the disparaging term for any people who, lacking acceptable genealogical credentials, were obviously of inferior caste.

About a thousand years ago, high status chiefs adventured from Ra'iatea outward in all directions. Legends tell how they sailed east to Tahiti, where they fought and conquered the Manahune of that island. To the west they subjugated the Manahune of what are now named the Cook Islands. The longest voyage was to those islands about 2,700 sailing miles to the north, now known as the Hawaiian Islands. Here, too, they found the descendants of earlier Polynesian discoverers. Over centuries of language change, "*manahune*" became "*menehune.*"

When the priest Pa'ao arrived in Hawai'i, he found no chiefs who, in his opinion, had the proper lineage to rule. Back he sailed to Ra'iatea, where he recruited Pili, a prince of the purest lineage. Returning to Hawai'i, Pa'ao installed Pili as king, and Pili founded the dynasty from which Kamehameha descended 28 generations later. Pa'ao established the new order by instituting new rites and building temples. At about the time William the Conqueror crossed the English Channel, Pa'ao logged not less than 11,000 miles on his voyages of conquest.

In the South Pacific, European explorers and missionaries heard certain commoners described as *manahune* or *mana'une.* The Hawaiian term for commoner, *maka'ainana,* may have originally distinguished commoners who came with the Tahitian chiefs from the Menehune who were already here.

A retreat by Menehune groups along the island chain would explain why Kauai, as their last holdout, has the most stories about them. Tales of the Menehune as living in the mountains but hungering for seafood suggest that they had been driven inland from the shore. It is also said that the Menehune king at last gave it up and sailed off to the west with most of his people. The fleet would have passed the islands of Necker and Nihoa, where several stone images have been found which are Polynesian in style but not typically Hawaiian.

A census of Kauai's people ordered by King Kaumuali'i in the early 19th century recorded 65 persons as being of Menehune ancestry.

Because conquerors often belittle or ignore their victims, or take credit for their achievements, the story of the original discovery of Hawai'i was quite likely obliterated by the Tahitian conquest. Existing tradition credits the discovery to a chief with the obviously mythical name Hawai'i-Loa.

Over the centuries Hawaiian memory of the Menehune became shrouded in mystery. Tales of those who lived in hiding in mountain forests became confused with myths of forest spirits, known throughout Polynesia as small beings, often invisible, and capable of doing great feats of work in a single night. The story of the boy Laka, as told in other Polynesian cultures, has him making his deal not with Menehune, but with forest spirits.

There is no distinctly Hawaiian tradition of the Menehune as a race of tiny people. They may have been 'little people' in the meaning used by politicians today when referring to the poor. Among Hawaiian historians, only Kamakau mentions them, and only as builders of temples.

When European writers heard about them, they may have interpreted "little" to mean small physical size rather than diminished social status. Such a mistake would have vastly amused their Hawaiian informants, who would have instantly seen the joke and enlarged upon it. Sensitive to what others wanted to hear, Polynesians have delighted in revamping and embellishing their stories to entertain non-Polynesian audiences. Such pranks, when discovered too late, have ruined ethnological studies and professional reputations. On Kauai,

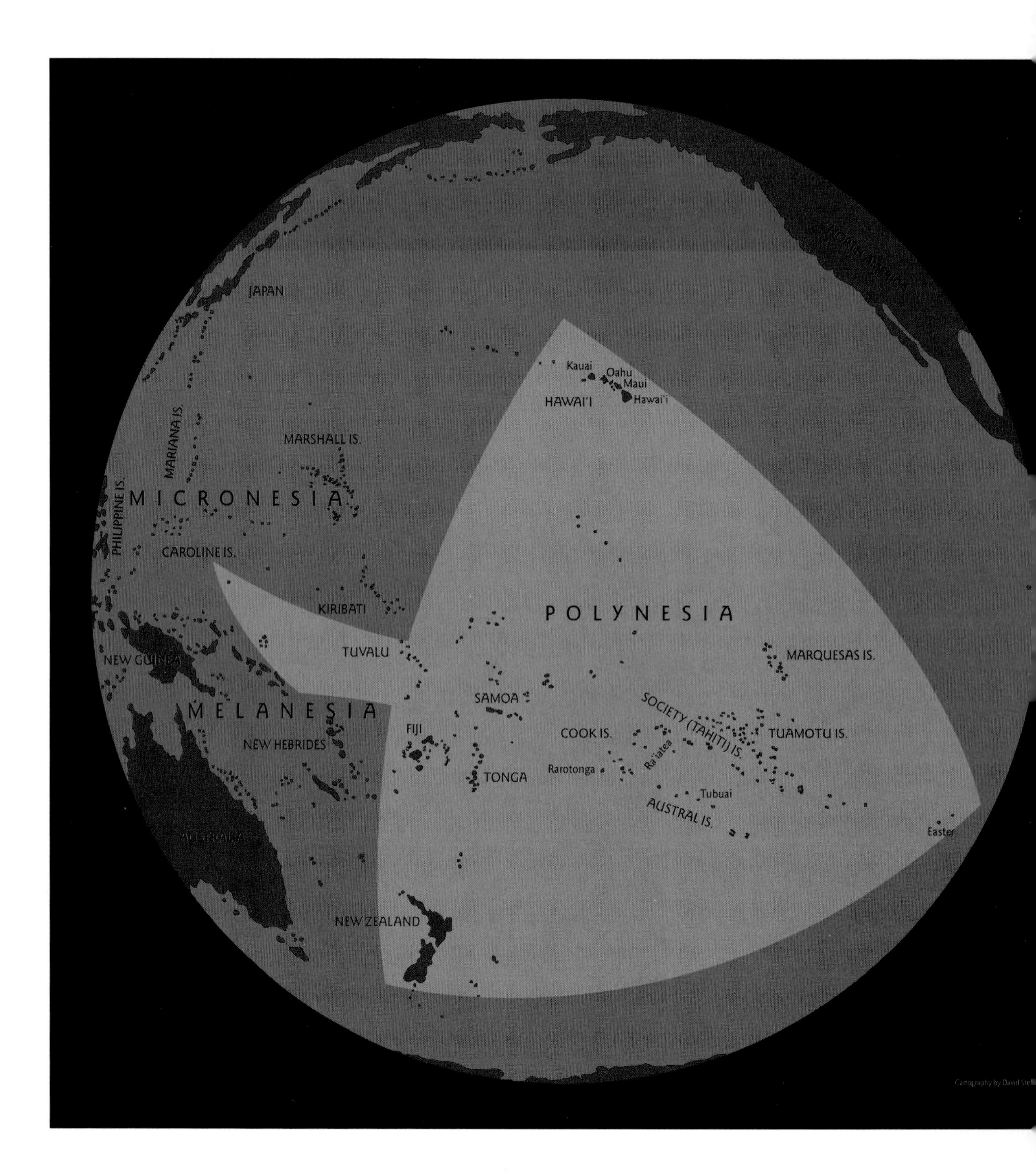

folklorist W.D. Rice was told about an ancient 'little people' by his Hawaiian informant Akina, and a new literary tradition of the myths of the Menehune, revised and enlarged edition, was born. To Akina it was, no doubt, hilarious fun.

By any standard, the achievement of the real Menehune was amazing.

At some time more than 1,900 years ago an expedition of sailing canoes, crafted without metal tools or fastenings, explored northward from some South Pacific island into an unknown sea. This could not have been an accidental drifting of storm-wrecked fishermen; the way north demanded close-reaching against the wind through three different regions of prevailing winds and ocean currents.Those who sailed would have been a chiefly family and loyal commoners, possibly exiled by famine or a lost battle. They knew the dangers, they knew of canoes which had sailed and never returned; but their ancestors had always found new islands in their ocean world, and the same ancestral spirits would guide them now. Moreover, careful observation of the flight paths of migratory land birds may have convinced them that land lay to the unexplored north.

The rising and setting places of stars were their compass, and the elevation of stars arching overhead indicated their latitude. During the day or on cloudy nights, they held their course by keeping their canoes consistently angled to a dominant ocean wave pattern. After a month at sea, the weather-worn navigators, possibly sighting the glare of a volcano in the night sky, found islands larger than any they had known.

Their landing, we may believe, was not without some ceremony to placate the spirits of this strange new land. They planted the cuttings and seeds which they had carried with them, and subsisted by fishing, bird hunting, and gathering until their first harvest was ready. And with great industry they made these islands a Polynesian place.

We know nothing of their traditions. We know not the names by which they knew themselves or their islands—only the names given by those who came centuries later. But we do know that they were Polynesian, both in stature and in courage, and deserve better than being known as *menehune*.

WHAT'S IN A NAME?

The Island of Hawai'i and its northern cape, Upolu Point, were apparently named by the "Tahitian" conquerors from Ra'iatea. Havai'i was the ancient, poetic name for Ra'iatea. Upolu was once the name for the small island at the northern end of the Ra'iatea lagoon, now known as Taha'a.

The ancient homeland of Eastern Polynesians was 'Havaiki in the West,' now thought to be the islands of Savai'i (formerly Havaiki or Havai'i), and Upolu, in the Samoan group.

In Samoa archaeologists have found evidence which dates discovery by a Proto-Polynesian people to more than 3,000 years ago. A trail of findings of a distinctive pottery leads westward from Samoa along the northern fringe of Melanesia, pointing to an ultimate origin in Southeast Asia. (notes: 9)

MOI'KEHA, THE VOYAGING KING
The Mo'ikeha Series is in the Collection of the Sheraton Coconut Beach Hotel, Kauai

THE MOʻIKEHA SAGA

"Behold, Hawaiʻi! An island, a people.
The people of Hawaiʻi
are the children of Tahiti!"

THUS BEGINS THE triumphant chant of Kamahuʻalele, navigator of the canoe of high chief Moʻikeha, composed when he first sighted the mountains of Hawaiʻi after a long return voyage from Tahiti.

Moʻikeha, with his brother Olopana and their mutual wife Luʻukia, had sailed from Waipiʻo Valley, Hawaiʻi to 'Tahiti of the Golden Haze,' not Tahiti Island but the leeward Tahitian islands of Raʻiatea, Bora Bora, and Huahine. Relatives welcomed them and gave them lands. Olopana went off on other adventures; some say he settled on Tahiti.

Luʻukia was a celebrated beauty, and her favors were sought by the chief Mua. To win her away from her husband, Mua whispered rumors of Moʻikeha's dalliances with other ladies. Furious, Luʻukia constructed a chastity belt of braided sennit, knotting it so intricately that Moʻikeha could not undo it. As the *paʻu o Luʻukia* (skirt of Luʻukia) it was later memorialized as the name of an extremely complicated sennit lashing by which the hulls of Hawaiian double canoes were fastened to connecting crossbeams.

Disgusted, Moʻikeha gathered his men and made the month-long return voyage to Hawaiʻi. He continued on to Kauai, where he lived for the remainder of his life, building his residence near Wailua Bay. He married the two daughters of the king, Puna, and upon Puna's death assumed the rule of the island.

KILA, THE SON
who avenged his father

KAHA'I, THE GRANDSON
who brought the breadfruit to Hawai'i

OLOPANA, THE BROTHER
ruling chief of Waipi'o, Hawai'i

KILA THE SON

In old age Mo'ikeha yearned for a son he had left in Tahiti, and chose his youngest son, Kila, to make the voyage. Kila sailed south. He found his half-brother La'a at a temple on Ra'iatea.

Kila's resemblance to his father was so striking that Lu'ukia fell in love with him at first sight. But Kila had other business in mind; he had learned of the slander by which the chief Mua had separated Lu'ukia from his father. He challenged Mua to a duel, and slew him.

KAHA'I THE GRANDSON

Kaha'i, grandson of Mo'ikeha, sailed to the South Pacific and returned bringing breadfruit plants. He landed at Kualoa at the northern end of Kaneohe Bay, Oahu.

Most breadfruit varieties will not grow from seed, but must be propagated as young sprouts that grow from the roots of trees. These are often difficult to move from one yard to the next. That they were kept alive and protected from deadly seawater on canoe voyages of thousands of miles attests to the agricultural skills of the Polynesians. Because Kaha'i is remembered for this feat, earlier attempts may not have succeeded.

Kualoa, now a Honolulu park, was once the site of summit meetings and ceremonies, chiefly residences, and a training ground for young chiefs; it was a place so sacred that passing canoes lowered their sails in salute.

In 1975, after the separate components of *Hokule'a* were built, it was our good fortune to

KAHA'I ENTERING KANEOHE BAY *Collection of Pentagram Corporation*

obtain the beach at Kualoa as a launching place. Here the assembly of the parts was done with lashings that consumed five miles of cordage, and the canoe was launched with traditional ceremony and feasting. And to Kualoa the canoe returned triumphant after its third South Pacific campaign in 1987.

GHOST STORY

Hokule'a's first trials were held outside of Kaneohe Bay. After a day of sailing, we were often able to catch a wave and surf back into the bay, a memorable experience in a sixty foot canoe. Years later, I painted Kaha'i's canoe entering Kaneohe Bay the same way.

The painting, a mural twenty feet long, was installed in Pentagram Corporation's Burger King restaurant in Kaneohe. About a year after the opening I received a telephone call from the Pentagram office in Honolulu. The manager of their Kaneohe restaurant, a newcomer to Hawai'i, had heard from several employees that the mural was "bothering" them, but they could not say how.

On the deck of the canoe in the painting stands a young woman, gazing forward at the mountains of Oahu. One night after all the employees had departed, he was closing the restaurant when, as he was about to turn out the lights, he happened to look out through the windows, and saw the same young woman, wearing the same skirt of fine matting, standing outside in the parking lot looking in at him. He turned toward the painting to confirm that it was the same girl. When he looked out the window again, she had disappeared.

When the story reached Pentagram Corporation the next day, partners Bob Pulley and John Finney decided to hold a Hawaiian blessing for the restaurant, something that had not been done at the time it opened. I was scheduled to be away on the date of the ceremony, but a friend, the entertainer George Kauhi (a.k.a. Zoulou), was present as my proxy. Later he called to say that the event was beautifully arranged and properly conducted, and that he felt that there would be no further occurrences of figures in the painting being seen out in the parking lot.

He has been right.

DID CANOES SHAPE THOSE WHO MADE THEM?

Back in my Chicago days, I sailed a racing catamaran on cold Lake Michigan with a friend whose dimensions were far more slender than mine. His teeth would begin to chatter long before I felt the same chill. When I remarked on this, he ungraciously attributed the difference to my insulating layer of fat.

Noting that Polynesians are larger and heavier than other tropical peoples, I was struck by the idea that their voyaging canoes, offering scant protection from wind and spray, could

THE BLIND NAVIGATOR OF TONGA
If this story seems fanciful, it is because Polynesian survival depended upon an intimacy with nature beyond the comprehension of modern attitudes. There are many tales like this, but this one is not legend, but history.

In 1820, when the Tongan fleet's navigators lost their way, Tuita Kahomovailahi asked his son to describe such signs as birds and clouds. Putting his arm into the sea, feeling the temperature and the pulse of the waves, he announced:

"Tell the King we are in Fijian waters."

"But where is land?" the navigators asked. The old man asked the position of the sun, then said:

"Tell the king that at noon he will see land."

At noon they sighted the Fijian island Lakemba.

have exerted selective pressures resulting in a shaping influence on the evolution of those who sailed them.

Proto-Polynesians found their way from Southeast Asia out to the mid-Pacific islands of Samoa and Tonga on a route that covered many islands and possibly several thousand years of repeated searches and settlements. On any island, when a chief had reason to leave and search farther eastward for new land, he would select companions who would give him the best chances of survival—large and strong enough to handle a canoe at sea, right it if capsized, and wield a war club if a landing had to be forced on a hostile shore. The demands made by the canoe upon those who would voyage in it would strongly influence his selection.

At sea, natural selection would cancel out any mistakes made on shore. Again the canoe's design, the best that could be done without metal tools or fastenings, would bring rigorous selective pressures on those who would sail in it, favoring for survival those with ample natural fat to insulate the body from the deadly chill of wind evaporation upon spray-drenched skin.

And when an uninhabited island was discovered, those who settled it would, in isolation, form the sole genetic pool for future explorations. Such conditions, repeated over many voyages of exploration and settlement, may explain the large physique that distinguishes Polynesians from other equatorial peoples.

I sent a note to Kenneth Emory at Bishop Museum. Was there any precedent in anthropology for the idea that an artifact may have shaped

READYING CANOES FOR A VOYAGE
Carefully wrapped sea rations of dried fish and fruits, breadfruit and taro paste, and water in gourds are stowed aboard. Young pigs, dogs, and chickens are selected for breeding stock. Early voyagers brought twenty four plant species to Hawai'i as seeds, cuttings, and young plants. Fine craftswork was taken as gifts should they find a hospitable shore, and weapons should they face hostility—as well as the tools required to implant a Polynesian culture on a newly-discovered island.

the physical evolution of those who had created it? Later, when I visited him in Honolulu his search of the scientific literature had produced only a paper suggesting that the *woomera,* or spear thrower, used over many thousands of years by Australia's Aboriginals, may have influenced their "linear development." Kenneth Emory liked the canoe idea, and I was flattered when he asked if he could publish it, which he did in *National Geographic,* December, 1974.

KUPE DISCOVERS NEW ZEALAND
The legendary discoverer Kupe sailed from Ra'iatea (then Havai'i), and returned to tell of a great land peopled only by birds. Others followed his sailing directions: "Keep to the left of the setting sun in November."

BATTLE AT RAROTONGA

The brothers Tangi'ia and Tutapu, chiefs of Ra'iatea, fought over hereditary rights. Tangi'ia fled in his canoe, but was relentlessly pursued by his angry brother. At sea he met and befriended a Samoan chief, Karika. They joined forces and sailed to Rarotonga. There Tutapu caught up with them and came storming ashore, but was slain in the fight that followed. Tangi'ia and Karika settled on Rarotonga and became ancestors of chiefs of that island.

KAUHI'S LAST STAND AT KA'ANAPALI
With those who chose to become his companions-in-death, the Maui chief Ka-uhi-'aimoku-a-Kama faces the combined forces of his brother Kamehameha Nui and Alapa'i, King of Hawai'i, at the conclusion of a long and bloody struggle for the rule of Maui. *Collection of Amfac/JMB*

HONAUNAU BAY
Sails down, fishing canoes return from sea in the stillness of a Kona sunset. In the background is the ancient Pu'uhonua (sanctuary) of Honaunau. Canoes are now powered by outboard engines. The sanctuary has become a national park.

A MANILA GALLEON OFF THE PUNA COAST OF HAWAI'I *Collection of Tim and Devon Guard*

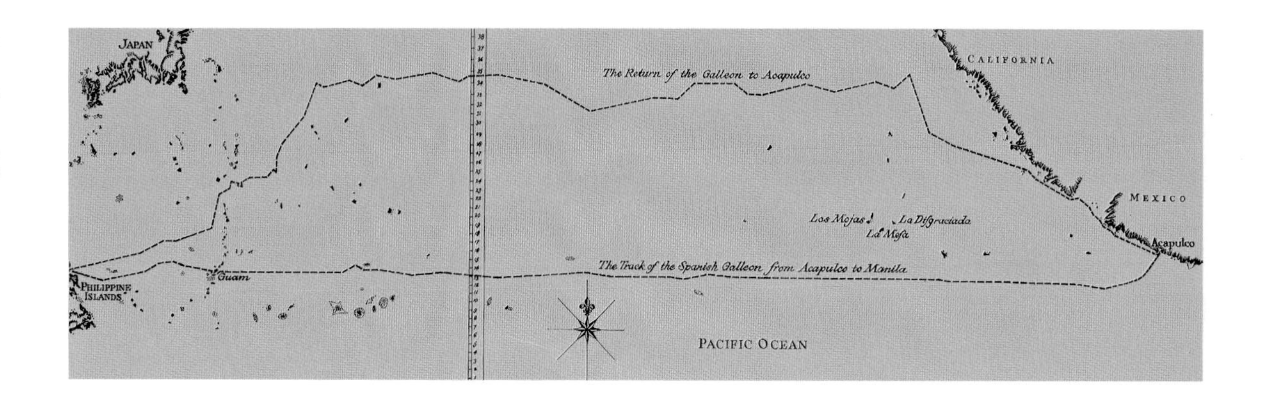

THE TRACK OF THE MANILA GALLEONS
Based on the British copy of the Spanish Chart captured by Anson. Unable to measure the strong westward current, the Spanish charted their sightings of the La Mesa group (Hawai'i) to the east of Hawai'i's true latitude.

THE MANILA GALLEONS

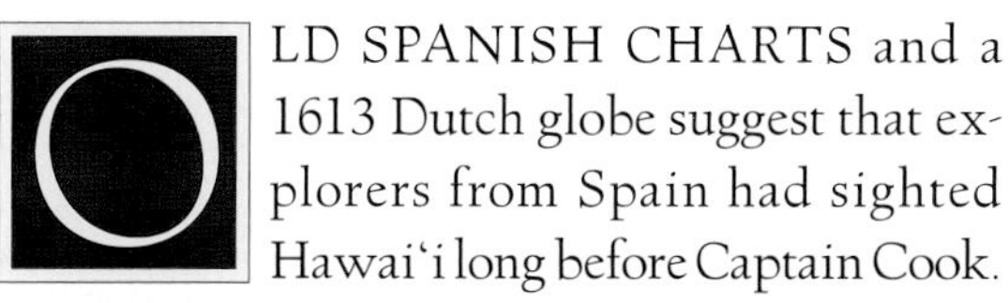

OLD SPANISH CHARTS and a 1613 Dutch globe suggest that explorers from Spain had sighted Hawai'i long before Captain Cook.

When Cook arrived in 1778, galleons laden with silver from the mines of Mexico and South America had been passing south of Hawai'i for two centuries on annual round trip voyages of 17,000 miles between Acapulco and Manila. The silver purchased spices, silks, porcelain and other riches of the Far East brought to Manila by Chinese traders. Loaded with these, the galleons sailed northward on monsoon winds until the latitude of prevailing westerlies was reached off Japan—winds which carried them back across the Pacific to Acapulco. There the goods were packed on burros across Mexico to Vera Cruz, shipped to Spain, then sold throughout Europe at great profit to the Spanish Crown.

Larger than the combined areas of all Earth's continents, the Pacific Ocean covers a third of the globe and spans nearly half the earth's circumference at the equator. Winds and ocean currents wheel through the North Pacific in a gigantic clockwise circuit. The discovery of this movement, gained at great sacrifice of ships and men, enabled the Spanish to set up this trade route by 1565.

It was a dangerous voyage. Six galleons were lost between 1600 and 1604, with an appalling loss of lives. The westbound trip averaged four months. Eastbound passages were still more hazardous, averaging six months. In the voyage northward to reach the westerlies off Japan lay the potential for destruction by typhoons. The remainder of the voyage meant facing storms of the North Pacific and eventually famine and disease. A tragic example of this pattern came when the *San Jose* sailed from Manila with more than 400 souls in 1657. Sighted nine months later near Acapulco, she did not answer signals. All aboard were found dead of starvation.

It seems improbable that Spanish mariners could have made several hundred trips on a route passing a few degrees south of Hawai'i without learning of its presence.

To protect their routes from the English—regarded with good reason as pirates—the Spanish cloaked their discoveries in the deepest secrecy. But rumors of the Manila galleons leaked out when English and Dutch adventurers began their own explorations in the Pacific. The Englishman Cavendish seized the *Santa Anna* in 1587 off Cape San Lucas, but without learning the ship's route.

The hero of James Clavell's novel *Shogun* was inspired by the adventures of Will Adams, the English pilot of a storm-wrecked Dutch expedition that landed at Japan in 1600 with only a few survivors. The Shogun of Japan valued Adams's talent as a navigator and ship-builder and gave him patronage. Over the objections of Portuguese missionaries and traders, Adams was able to establish English and Dutch trading stations in Japan—discontinued soon after his death.

In 1609 the galleon *San Francisco,* carrying the governor of Manila to Mexico, was wrecked on the coast of Japan. Here the governor waited for a year until a ship which Adams had built for the shogun was given to him. Through such contacts the English became aware of the Spanish trade route. Attacks on the galleons, however, were often repulsed. English cannonballs bounced off the hardwood sheathing of their hulls. In one battle, the *Sanctisima Trinidad* was struck by 1,000 rounds, but none of the cannon balls penetrated her sides. In all, only four galleons were lost to capture.

A century later, with England and Spain conveniently at war, the English captain George Anson persuaded his superiors to send him out after a Manila galleon. Less than enthusiastic, they gave him ships, some of doubtful seaworthiness, and made him wait nine months for men and supplies. His request for "seasoned" troops was answered with a cruel joke—old and infirm veterans from the military hospitals, some of whom had to be carried aboard. None survived Anson's later difficulties in the Pacific.

Most of his ships failed even to round Cape Horn, and turned back. Anson and his men recuperated on an uninhabited Pacific island—then did some raiding as he worked northward along the coast of South America. Word reached Acapulco, and when he was seen offshore the Spanish held the galleon in port. Anson decided on a daring stratagem—to cross the Pacific and ambush the galleon in the Philippines.

Only the flagship *Centurion* survived the crossing, with severe storm damage and loss of life from scurvy. Anson repaired his ship in China, filled out his ravaged crew with Chinese sailors, returned to the Philippines, and waited off the island of Samar.

The Spanish sent out two galleons in 1743. Anson missed the first but caught the second. The *Nuestra Senora de Covadonga,* unprepared for an attack, was captured in a bloody battle.

Centurian limped back to England in an almost sinking condition, but with more gold and silver than existed in the treasury. As might be expected, Anson was knighted and put in charge of the Navy. (notes: 10)

On the galleon he found a *"chart of all the ocean, between the Philippines and the coasts of Mexico."* On it was a cluster of islands in mid-ocean. Of these, the island La Mesa is on the latitude of the Island of Hawai'i, and its southern contour resembles the southern coastline of Hawai'i. *Mesa* aptly describes the long, massive shape of the major mountain, Mauna Loa. That the islands of the group are not in the correct relative positions to each other may be the composite result of multiple sightings over many years, each captain charting his discovery according to his guess of longitude.

Longitude was the historic problem for navigators. Latitude could be found with simple instruments measuring the altitude of Polaris above the horizon, or the sun's altitude at noon. But not until the development in 1744 of the chronometer, an accurate, portable timepiece, could longitude (distance in degrees east-west) be more than a guess, reckoned by the distances which the ship had covered within periods of time according to estimates of the ship's speed during each period.

Speed was measured with a block of wood attached to a line on which knots were tied at intervals. This 'log' was cast from the stern, and the number of knots that had run out during a

A WARRIOR CHIEF OF OLD HAWAI'I *Collection of Michael Warren*

certain time enabled the navigator to calculate the speed of the ship. The terms 'log' and 'knots' are survivors of that era.

But this method could not measure the force of the west-bound ocean current. Consequently, any island sighted would probably have been charted to the east of its true position. The islands on Spanish charts were variously 9 to 13 degrees east of Hawai'i's longitude.

Captain Cook, equipped with the first chronometer ever seen in the North Pacific, was able to accurately determine the longitude of the Hawaiian Islands. Naming them for the Earl of Sandwich, he placed them on the map of his voyage with the Spanish islands positioned to the east. Seven years later the French explorer La Perouse, sailing from California to Hawai'i, reckoned his longitude both by the old method and the new, and found the difference to be 6 degrees. His ships were fast frigates. The slower galleons, in the same strong current, would have produced an error of at least 10 degrees. In his journal La Perouse wrote: "*In the charts might be written: Sandwich Islands, surveyed in 1778 by Captain Cook, who named them, but anciently discovered by the Spanish navigators.*"

James Burney, one of Cook's officers, later an admiral and a leading expert on navigation and astronomy, calculated the error in Spanish charts at 9 degrees, and concluded that the La Mesa group were indeed the Sandwich Islands.

The same cluster of small islands appears at Hawai'i's latitude on a terrestrial globe built in 1613 by Jodocus Hondius and Adrian Veen of Amsterdam for Spanish clients, now housed at the National Maritime Museum, Greenwich, England. Converting the globe's longitude to the modern equivalent, I found the longitude of the largest island to be approximately 10 degrees east of the longitude of Hawai'i.

Although the westward track of the galleons passed south of Hawai'i by several hundred miles, the glow of a volcanic eruption in the night sky may have lured a curious captain northward into view of the major island. Those blown off their track by a storm would, as they sailed westward, have sighted the major Hawaiian islands at anywhere from 19 to 23 degrees North—a target impossible to miss.

Several reasons may be given for Spanish failure to establish a station in these islands:

The large and unwieldy galleons required safe and spacious natural harbors, but none existed in the Hawaiian Islands except Honolulu harbor, which could not be seen from offshore and was not known to Europeans until 16 years after Cook's arrival.

The Spanish carried a huge supply of water from Acapulco and had no need to stop at Hawai'i for that necessity.

Spanish landings would have been hotly contested. Polynesians were almost always hostile at first contact with Europeans arriving in threatening numbers. Departing from Acapulco in March, the Spanish would not have had Cook's good fortune to arrive in the winter months of makahiki when Hawaiian warfare was out of season. Moreover, galleon captains were under strict orders to take no risks that might endanger their precious cargoes. They were on business trips, not explorations. The sighting of strange islands would be of cartographic interest, but landing on them was quite another matter.

And, had they managed to establish peaceful contact, the Spanish would have found no gold, silver, or gems to catch their interest.

Cook's officers were convinced that the Spanish had preceded them. At Kauai, Captain Clerke saw "many Iron Utensils," but described only some skewer-like iron daggers and a broken sword. A stone image collected later in the 18th century, now in a German museum, appears to wear the ruff collar of a Spanish noble. Brown hair among Hawaiians has been attributed to Spanish genes, but this occurs among all Polynesians. Any biological imprint made by a few Spanish sailors on the Hawaiian gene pool would have certainly disappeared after several generations of intermarriage.

Early Christian missionaries to Hawai'i heard tales of strangers who had arrived long before the British. The missionary Rev. William Ellis was told of seven foreigners who had landed eight generations earlier at Kealakekua Bay in a painted boat with an awning or canopy over the stern. They were dressed in clothing of white and yellow, and one wore a long knife at his side and a feather in his hat. Upon landing they prostrated themselves in prayer. They were treated kindly, and lived out their lives in Hawai'i. Another story told of light-skinned strangers who landed on Hawai'i and retreated to the mountains. The Hawaiians gave them gifts, but the strangers kept to themselves and later sailed away. (notes: 11)

But could these visitors have been Europeans? Asians? Only if we can believe that all were completely free of those diseases which were unknown in Hawai'i until the arrival of the Cook expedition; or that the strangers refrained —or were isolated—from physical contact with the population.

The history of first contacts between Polynesians and Europeans suggests that a Spanish landing in force would likely have been forcibly stopped at the water's edge, but a few helpless survivors of a shipwreck would have been shown mercy. The pre-Cook absence of disease argues that such earlier arrivals either kept to themselves—as in the second tale—or were isolated in the same way that Hawaiians isolated their caste of 'untouchable' slaves. (notes: 12)

Within the Archive of the Indies in Seville are cabinets containing many thousands of documents pertaining to Spanish activities in the Americas and the Pacific. Sealed by order of the Crown, many of these have not been opened for centuries. But some day, opened under the light of scholarship, they may reveal the stories of those who gave the names La Mesa, Las Monges, La Desgraciada, and La Vestina to the forgotten islands on the Spanish charts. (notes: 13)

CROSSING TO MOLOKAI
A canoe struggles across the Kaiwi Channel. When powerful ocean swells bounce off the islands and collide in mid channel, they can heap up to great size. On such days, the waters between the Hawaiian Islands can become as rough as any in the tropics. *Collection of Kimo Austin*

RESOLUTION

MOMENT OF CONTACT
Left: The Cook Expedition off Kauai, 1778
Collection of the Kauai Westin Resort

KING KAHEKILI APPROACHING *DISCOVERY* OFF MAUI
Right: The Surgeon's mate Samwell wrote:
"In the afternoon Ka-he-kere the King of this Island & of another which we saw to Leeward called Morotai came on board the Discovery in a large double Canoe attended by a large Train dressed in red feathered Cloaks and Caps. As the Canoe approached the Ship one man stood up and waved his Cloak about his Head while the rest sung in concert much after the manner of the Otaheiteans."
Collection of Tim and Devon Guard

This imagery has also been developed as a mural for Pentagram Corporation, installed in the Burger King restaurant, Kahului, Maui.

MOMENT OF CONTACT

"H*ow do we account for this Nation spreading itself so far over this Vast ocean?"* Thus wrote Captain James Cook upon meeting the many people of the Hawaiian island of Kauai, a people of the same "*Nation*" and language as the peoples of New Zealand, Easter Island, Tonga, and Tahiti.

On his third Pacific voyage, Cook sailed north from Tahiti with orders to explore the northwestern coast of North America. The expedition arrived off Nawiliwili Bay, Kauai, on January 19, 1778. Fishermen in canoes were seen coming from the shore. Cook backed the main yard to await them, and hailed them in his imperfect Tahitian.

"*It required but little address to get them to come along side, but we could not prevail upon any one to come on board; they exchanged a few fish they had in the Canoes for any thing we offered them, but valued nails, or iron above every other thing; the only weapons they had were a few stones in some of the Canoes and these they threw overboard when they found they were not wanted.*" (notes: 14)

Cook sailed westward along the southern shore of Kauai, purchasing "*roasting pigs and some very fine potatoes*" from other canoes which came out, and anchoring that evening in Waimea Bay. After trading for provisions and water on Kauai and Ni'ihau, he continued northward toward Alaska, naming the islands after his patron, the Earl of Sandwich. He would return to the Sandwich Islands ten months later.

Despite firm orders to avoid contact with women, his men had left venereal disease. On the flogging list we find "*Will Bradyley, for disobeying orders, with two dozen* [lashes], *and having connections with women knowing himself to be injured, with the Venereal disorder.*" Cook was sorrowful about this, knowing that just one Bradyley was enough to infect an entire race.

OFF MAUI, 1778

When the Arctic winter drove Cook back to the Sandwich Islands, the expedition was in desperate need of provisions and repairs. His ships, *Resolution* and *Discovery*, appeared off windward Maui in November, 1778.

King Kahekili came off shore in a large canoe, his men all wearing feather capes and singing. He boarded *Discovery*, and the first chief in his retinue convinced Captain Clerke that he had been aboard that ship when it had anchored at Kauai. Venereal disease had also reached Maui, as evidenced by the suffering of one of the chiefs who "*spoke of the Isle Atowi* [Kauai] *as if we had left it in that place the last year.*"

Cook plied offshore, trading for food and water brought out in canoes, and working to windward along the Maui coast. Off Hana, he was visited by an elderly ruling chief who brought gifts and invited him to land. Cook declined, but accepted sailing directions to the next island, Hawai'i, where he was told he would "*meet with good People & plenty of refreshments.*" Cook would not know until seven weeks later that this chief was Kalaniopu'u, the king of Hawai'i Island, who had been prosecuting his

THE COOK EXPEDITION OFF WAIPI'O VALLEY, HAWAI'I
Collection of Samuel A. Cooke

VISITORS FROM ANOTHER WORLD

Right: Leaving a village, the makahiki procession pauses on Hawai'i's rugged southeastern shore to gaze at Cook's *Resolution*, also making a circuit of the island. At this time Clerke's *Discovery* was far behind and out of sight. The bearer in the foreground holds the *akua loa*, the standard of Lono. In the village the *akua pa'ani*, standard of the god of sports and games, has been set up, and festivities are about to begin.
Collection of Jewel Rose

fourth unsuccessful campaign against Maui, a war now canceled by the makahiki, an annual season during which warfare was out of season.

COOK ENTERING KEALAKEKUA BAY
An incomplete painting of the arrival of the Cook expedition at Kealakekua Bay, January 1779.
Photo by Lee Allen Thomas

H.M.S. *RESOLUTION*
Cook's flagship on his second and third Pacific voyages. *Right: Resolution* was a sturdy "Whitby Cat" built for hauling coal. Small but roomy, maneuverable, shallow drafted, such ships were well suited for explorations. This ship was 462 tons burden, 110' in hull length, 31' in breadth, and armed with 12 four-pounder cannon and 12 swivel guns. Shoddy refitting at the Navy Yard resulted in failures and leaking that plagued the third voyage. When a rotten foremast gave way, Cook was forced to return to Kealakekua Bay, where he met his death.
Collection of William and Sarah Green

AROUND HAWAI'I THE HARD WAY

A swift canoe must have preceded the expedition, because "*pigs, fruit, and roots*" in good supply were readily brought out in canoes upon Cook's arrival off Hawai'i.

Much to the dismay of his weary men, Cook chose not to sail comfortably downwind into the lee of Hawai'i. Instead, he worked slowly upwind along the windward shore, making long bruising tacks, never landing, pausing only to trade for provisions brought out in canoes. His ships were battered and leaking, his men by his own account "*mutinous*." The flogging list lengthened as Cook's temper shortened. After nearly going on the rocks while rounding the eastern cape of Hawai'i, he put the wind astern and coasted down the southern shore.

At the same time, the annual makahiki procession was making its circuit around the island. Makahiki was the season of Rono (pronounced Lono today), god of the land and agriculture. A harvest festival and a time for tax-gathering, makahiki also marked the change of the year, when the invisible Rono returned to repossess the land as his wife, inseminating it with rain and renewing its fertility. From late October to early February the power of the god Ku, patron of the works of men, was held in abeyance. No major project of work or warfare requiring the patronage of Ku could be attempted. Having usurped the land during the rest of the year so

RESOLUTION

that they could plant it and make a living from it, men now released the land back to Rono so that it might be restored. (notes: 15)

Each year a procession went around the island carrying the Rono standard—a long pole with banners of *tapa* (barkcloth), feather pennants, ferns, and imitation birds hanging from a cross-piece. In each district gifts of craftwork and food were brought to this standard as gifts to Rono. But just as men usurped the land from the god, the gifts were taken by the chiefs, some to be kept as taxes, the rest to be distributed back to the people. Makahiki festivities included a mock battle by which men ritually repossessed the land, driving those carrying the Rono standard—symbolizing Rono—out of the district. At the close of makahiki, the temples were once again consecrated to Ku.

At this time the British began hearing Hawaiians referring to Cook as "Rono." This has been taken to mean that Cook was seen as the god Rono; but David Malo, a scholar raised in Kamehameha's court, suggested that the name was derived from the similarity of the *tapa* banners that hung from the Rono standard to the square sails of Cook's ships.

KEALAKEKUA BAY

Rounding the southern cape of Hawai'i, the British were escorted by a growing number of canoes as they sailed north along the leeward side of the island. Cook entered the island's one safe anchorage, Kealakekua Bay, after his sailing master, William Bligh, went ahead in a small boat and was shown a good anchorage and a spring of fresh water. The ships were escorted into the bay by an estimated 1,000 canoes, with 10,000 persons being on the water in canoes, on surfboards, and swimming "like shoals of fish." The king was away, but two pleasant young chiefs officiated as harbor masters. An elderly priest escorted Cook ashore to a temple built upon a large rock platform beside the beach. Here a complicated ceremony was performed which mystified the British, one in which Cook was again addressed as "Rono".

Rono, it was learned, was a title of high chiefly status, but one which apparently carried little executive power—just the thing to award an obviously important and potentially dangerous visitor. At Kealakekua the British were entertained by a high chief whose name they heard as "Omeah," but who was also referred to as "Rono" and paid the same honors given to Cook, including prostration by commoners while in his presence.

When the king appeared nine days later with a huge fleet of canoes, the British were surprised to discover that this was the same elderly chief they had met off Maui. After a visit with Cook, he retired to his residence.

The next morning the king cleared the bay of canoe traffic, then came out with three large canoes. The first carried the king and many chiefs, and was laden with brilliant feather capes. The second carried priests and large feather-covered spirit-images, and the third was heavily loaded with provisions. A stately procession was made around Cook's ships, perhaps the most impressive spectacle the British had seen in the Pacific.

KING KALANIOPU'U WELCOMES COOK WITH A CANOE PROCESSION AT KEALAKEKUA BAY
Nine days after the British dropped anchor the king arrived from Maui with his war fleet. The following morning he cleared the bay of all traffic, then made a formal procession around Cook's ships with three large canoes. Cook then followed him ashore for an exchange of gifts.
Collection of Jay Rose

RESOLUTION

Cook followed the king ashore, and many gifts were exchanged.

In Polynesia, any gift, whether of goods or service, obliged the receiver to reciprocate. The lavish hospitality offered to the British suggests that the king wanted a large favor in return. Having failed on four attempts to satisfy his one great obsession, a conquest of Maui, the idea of enlisting Cook as an ally could not have eluded him. To shower a European captain with hospitality, then invite him to bring along his guns in a lovely little war against another island, was a routine tactic of Pacific island chiefs, dating from the very beginning of European exploration when Magellan joined such an adventure and got himself killed.

Having no writing by Cook's hand after the moment of entering Kealakekua Bay, we have no confirmation of this theory; we may be certain, however, that he would have firmly refused such a request, much to the king's disappointment. The chiefs began asking the British when they were going to leave.

DEATH SCENE

Soon after Cook's departure, a rotten foremast footing gave way in a gale. Knowing of no other harbor, he reluctantly returned to the bay to make repairs. The British had learned nothing of makahiki, but that season had now ended, and the king was immersed in the rituals by which he—representing man— resumed his discipline over the land. Kalaniopu'u's vast displeasure at Cook's untimely return suggests that the British were now seen as a political threat.

THE DEATH OF COOK, FEBRUARY 14, 1779

This event became a popular subject of European painters—each successive painting being more fanciful than the last. Even Webber, artist with the expedition, took license with the event. His oil painting, done after his return to England, depicts Cook dressed up for the event in formal breeches and hose, whereas an earlier sketch showed him wearing the more customary canvas trousers. Webber painted Cook being attacked while standing on a sandy beach; but Cook was struck down while striding toward the water across a broad shelf of lava.

This painting is an attempt to reconstruct the moment more accurately. It is based on the accounts of those who were present, a study of the weapons and dress of both sides, and estimates by scientists of the physical setting.

In this painting may be the first depiction of the Hawaiian battle mat. British journals refer to the bulky protective mats worn by Hawaiian warriors, but there are no existing mats, or drawings showing how they were fashioned and worn. The best clue was found in Lt. King's statement that these were worn in the same manner as the feather capes, and both King and Clerke described the feather capes as battle apparel.

Knowing that in close combat the cape was shifted from behind and carried over the left shoulder, with the bulk of the cape held forward by the left hand to take the impact of a sling stone or to snag the point of a spear or dagger, and leaving the right shoulder and arm exposed and free to wield a weapon, we may assume that the battle mat was worn the same way.

Geologists believe that this coastline has subsided 28 inches in the last 200 years. The rock from which Cook fell is now submerged, but one may still locate it and study it through a diver's mask. I had help from Marine Advisor Pete Hendricks— computer work following moon phases backward in time produced an estimate of the tide at 8:00 AM, 14 February, 1779. With this data the waterline could be depicted on the rock with some confidence.

Marine Lt. Molesworth Phillips heard Cook's last shout, but then lost sight of Cook in the confusion. He was struck down and stabbed in the shoulder, but managed to raise himself and fire at his assailant before escaping. Witnesses saw a man with a fencepost or crude club strike Cook behind the head, while a chief in a feather cape rushed around a parked double canoe and stabbed him with one of the iron daggers the ship's blacksmiths had been forging as trade items.

This man was known to the British as "Nua" (probably Kanuha), a close relative of the king, who Surgeon's Mate Samwell described as a chief of "*... great consequence ... tall and stout and one who united in his figure the two qualities of strength and agility in a greater degree, than I ever remembered to have seen before in any other man.*" Cook fell. Face down in the water, he was stabbed many times.

In the painting, at the far left, the old king is being taken away to safety. The boy fleeing in the foreground represents the king's son who happened to be sitting in one of the boats when the fracas began. The marine corporal, James Thomas, is depicted waist deep in the water, receiving a mortal wound from a dagger thrust. *Resolution* is shown with the foremast removed; it had been hoisted out and taken to the beach at the other side of the bay for repair.

Cook's hand was raised toward the boats. This gesture has been widely interpreted as a signal to his men to cease firing. However, J.C. Beaglehole, the most eminent of Cook scholars, found no justification for this belief. Cook was waving to the boats to come in closer to shore. Like so many mariners of his day, he could not swim.

Collection of Christopher Hemmeter

Incited by their chiefs, commoners began testing British mettle with thievery and teasing. After the theft of a blacksmith's tongs, British sailors retaliated by taking a canoe, but were beaten in the ensuing scuffle. To the merriment of commoners who no longer prostrated themselves in his presence, Cook was led on a false chase after the thief. Furious, he resolved to use firearms to regain his prestige.

This was not the same diplomatic and self-disciplined Cook of earlier voyages, but a man whose behavior was now affected by illness and exhaustion. British diaries show that in the last months of his life, he was given to erratic reactions, flaring into foot-stamping tantrums at slight provocations, flogging his men for petty offenses. (Notes: 16)

When a boat which had been moored to *Discovery* was missing at dawn, February 14th, he ordered cannon fired at canoes and sent out armed boats to cordon off the bay. He then went ashore with marines, planning to invite the king to his ship, then to take him hostage against the return of the boat.

Ashore, his plan was thwarted by the king's bodyguards. Cook was retiring to the boats when word came that a boat stationed across the bay had fired on a canoe and killed an important chief. There was a shout of outrage. Men hastily armed themselves. At a menacing gesture Cook fired both barrels of his musket, then ordered the marines to fire. But the king's guards charged into the smoke, killing Cook and four marines. His last words were "Take to the boats!"

Fire from the boats and cannon fire from *Resolution* cleared the rocky shore, but not before Hawaiians had retrieved, as a custom of honor, the four chiefs and thirteen commoners who had been killed. When the British made no move to land, the Hawaiians dashed forward and took the British dead as well.

Cook's corpse was given the mortuary treatment of a high chief, in which the flesh was disposed of at sea and the bones carefully cleaned and preserved in plaited reliquaries. Some of the flesh was turned over to the British when they requested the return of Cook's body. The horror expressed by Hawaiians when asked the "direct question" satisfied the British that the Hawaiians were not cannibals. Later, when some sailors got out of control on the other side of the bay, burning houses and killing the people of an undefended area, then impaling several heads on poles and bringing these out to the ships, Captain Clerke had the heads buried at sea in front of Hawaiian witnesses so that the Hawaiians would not think that the British were cannibals.

Clerke, although ill with tuberculosis that would kill him in a few months, managed to restore order among his men. Genial and well-liked, he repaired relations with his hosts, and when the ships sailed away a cordiality had been established. In his journal he noted that from the beginning he had been offered the same honors that were given to Cook, honors which have led historians to believe that the Hawaiians saw Cook as their god Rono. But Clerke had always refused them, writing in his journal: "*I disliked exceedingly putting so many people to such confounded inconvenience.*"

POLYNESIAN MERMAID

Collection of Paul and Elaine Barton

The sexual appetites of Cook's men, most of whom were in their 'teens or twenties, were matched by the eagerness of "the lower class" of Polynesian girls to prove their feminine prowess by making sexual conquests—a cultural trait that British seamen were quick to exploit. Surgeons mate David Samwell wrote many glowing descriptions of "the dear girls."

Once Cook knew that "the venereal distemper" had been passed to a native population, he allowed women on the ships day and night—unlike the Spanish in Tahiti, or the Russians in Alaska, who apparently avoided sexual contact with non-Christian women.

Samwell wrote that the Spanish "*... will always be looked upon with Contempt by the lovely Nymphs of Otaheite ... they frequently complained to us of this unmanly Behaviour of the flesh-subduing Dons. We gave them every consolation in our power ... blind Sinners that we are.*"

At Tonga: "*...we saw great Numbers of Girls here as beautiful or more so than any at Otaheite & who in symmetry and proportion might dispute the palm with any women under the Sun.*"

At Hawaii: "*The beautiful Nymphs of Owhyhee make that which is the chief object of their pleasure the general Subject of their Discourse, & feel no Shame in inviting you to their Embraces by lascivious Gestures and every female blandishment. They have in general handsome faces and are very well made ... they are very clean, have good Teeth and are perfectly void of any disagreeable Smell.*"

How Polynesians, who bathed at every opportunity, could bear standing downwind of 18th century Europeans, much less embracing them, Samwell does not discuss. In a letter to a friend he expresses an opinion that was universal among British seamen:

"*The Natives of all the South Sea Islands...are a good natured humane & well disposed People in my opinion much superior to ourselves in those respects—the Women are well made, exceedingly clean and have very beautiful Faces, when we add to this that they are universally goodnatured and of a merry agreeable Disposition & always possessed of a good Flow of Spirits, what the Devil can we wish for more, till we get to Heaven.*"

HOW COOK BECAME A GOD

The diaries kept by the British offer no direct evidence that Cook was seen by Hawaiians as the god Rono. The myth of Cook as a Hawaiian god originated not in Hawai'i, but in Britain several years after Cook's death.

Britain's fortunes were at low ebb. The American Colonies were in revolt, the public had lost confidence in the government, and the king's health was in decline. Survival of the empire demanded a role model for future generations of empire builders. Cook, having raised himself from the humblest of origins to national prominence by virtue of his skill and accomplishments, was the perfect choice.

His posthumous reputation was promoted beyond the restraints of history and fashioned into legend. The legend invoked a hero's death in the classic mode—not a death in a dirty little skirmish with mere savages, but death at the hands of savages who, by accepting him as their god, were transformed into instruments of fate.

In all mythologies fate decrees that heroes who rise too rapidly, who approach too close to godliness, must be struck down. It is an ancient and universal theme, striking some primordial chord. At this time the Classical Revival was sweeping Europe, with a mythical, romanticized view of the cultures of Ancient Greece and Rome acting as a touchstone for the arts. Cook, the great explorer, was now a national hero deserving of a hero's death in the classic mode. For Britain, reshaping the story of Cook's death would create a myth for a new era, for a manifest destiny of the British as the enlightened shapers of a brave new world. (Notes: 17)

It was perhaps at this moment that Western man began to remold his mythology of the past into a mythology of the future.

There are significant differences between the shipboard journals kept by Cook and his men and the official account of the voyage published several years later. Cook's journal was edited for publication with much rewriting by the Rev. John Douglas. For an account of events that followed the end of Cook's journal, Lieutenant James King, now promoted to Captain, was hired. King rewrote his earlier account, making revisions which seem calculated to suggest that Cook was seen as a supernatural being. One obvious deletion by King was an incident during the ceremony at the temple when Cook, at the request of the priests, prostrated himself before the image of the god Ku-nui-akea and kissed it.

After publication of the official account of the voyage, any pamphlet, picture, or teapot bearing Cook's name or portrait found an insatiable market. Print shops were flooded with demand for popular engravings in which the myth was given graphic form. One, titled *The Apotheosis of Captain Cook,* depicts the great navigator being lifted by the female figures of Britannia and a trumpeting angel above billowing clouds of gunsmoke at Kealakekua Bay. At least six paintings were done of his death, each more fanciful than the last. Theatrical performances about Cook were mobbed. He was praised from pulpits in sermons which a few centuries earlier might have brought him sainthood.

If Hawaiians have had difficulty with the idea that their ancestors saw Cook as an incarnation of the god Rono, it is because there had been no precedent for it. High chiefs may have been revered as descendants of gods; but, as the British were informed at Kealakekua Bay, the great gods were invisible and dwelt in the heavens. The mythical period when these deities walked the earth was ancient and remote to the Hawaiians of 1778. Their society, was based on static concepts, placing great value on preserving the status quo. Without precedent, the idea that Cook might be one of their major gods could not have been imagined.

CONDEMNATION OF COOK BY MISSIONARIES

Hawaiian memory of Cook's visits was not seriously documented until a half century later, when such memory had become confused with the visits of others. When the American missionaries decided to publish their history of Hawai'i, Hawaiian students were sent out to gather information. Unfortunately, the anglophobic American missionary Sheldon Dibble got his hands on it, rewriting the work to cast Cook, as well as the original Hawaiian culture, in the worst possible light.

Humiliated by the War of 1812, Americans nursed a grudge against Britain. Eager to establish influence in Hawai'i, but frustrated by the strong friendship of the Hawaiian Monarchy toward Britain, Americans were eager for anything that might discredit Britain in Hawaiian eyes. Dibble seized on the myth not to praise Cook, but to condemn him for self-deification, a blasphemy by which Cook supposedly incurred the wrath of the Almighty and brought about his own death.

Dibble also accused Cook of deliberately permitting his men to infect the people with venereal disease, and himself bedding down with a Hawaiian princess. But Cook never touched native women—on that point the journals of his men, including those most critical of him, are unanimous. And the princess, who we are told was Lelemahoalani of Kauai, was no more than eight years old at the time.

Other American missionaries joined with enthusiasm in the denunciation. Their published version of Hawaiian history, taught with venom to generations of Hawaiian students, created among Hawaiians a feeling of revulsion toward Cook that persists today. (Notes: 18)

HISTORY'S DEBT TO COOK

By the late 18th century, European contact with Hawai'i had become as inevitable as its disastrous consequences to a disease free people. But those who seek to improve their view of the original civilization of these islands are fortunate that the opening of Hawai'i to Europe was made by the relatively sympathetic and articulate members of the Cook expedition, men who were trained as observers by their mentor. As they readily confess in their writings, they could not comprehend much of what they witnessed; but they were good enough to set down their observations in writings and drawings. These records give us a window to a past which, had the first contact been made by illiterate traders or pirates, might have been closed to us forever.

THE COOK EXPEDITION AT WAIMEA, OAHU

The first recorded European contact with the island of Oahu was made after Cook's death when the expedition, now under Captain Charles Clerke's command, landed at Waimea Bay in late February, 1779.

Passing eastern and northern Oahu, Clerke saw "... *by far the most beautiful Country we have yet seen among these Isles ... bounteously cloath'd with Verdure, on which were situate many large Villages and extensive Plantations.*"

The British landed, were kindly received, collected water from "a pleasing murmuring river", and departed, luckily before Waimea's famous surf came up. Most of the chiefs and many of the men happened to be away prosecuting a war on Molokai.

Waimea Valley today is the site of Waimea Falls Park, a delightful *kaulana* (place of rest and recreation) wherein many of the ancient historical, cultural, and botanical attributes of Hawai'i are preserved.

Collection of Charles Pietsch III

WEBBER'S INCOMPLETE SKETCH *Courtesy of the Bishop Museum, Honolulu*

WEBBER'S WATERCOLOUR *Courtesy of the Dixson Library, Sydney*

MASKED PADDLERS AT KEALAKEKUA BAY

The painting that took 200 years to complete

John Webber, artist with Captain Cook in Hawai'i, was only 24 years old when the expedition left England. Trained to represent the human figure in the idealized 'classical' proportions and poses then popular in Europe, he encountered some difficulty depicting the physiques of Polynesians; but he had a remarkable eye for detail, sympathy for his subjects, and the drawing ability of a mature artist.

By studying his work, I've come to know and like the person it reveals; and, if I could be certain of meeting him in that Great Studio, I would look forward with much relish to the interview. No doubt he would be astonished to learn how important his drawings have become as a window to the original Hawaiian culture. His was the role of those artists, in all times, whose depictions convey a vital sense of history that would otherwise lie buried in words.

From the deck of *Resolution* as it lay at anchor in Kealakekua Bay, Webber saw a small double canoe moving under both sail and paddles toward the beach at the eastern side of the bay. As it passed by, he had only a moment to sketch in a few pencil lines. He added some details and a few washes of watercolor. Then for some reason he abandoned this attempt, and, working at his drawing table sometime later, started afresh on another piece of paper.

He completed this second effort as a watercolor, but made some significant changes from his earlier sketch, introducing errors in the construction and rigging of the canoe, greatly reducing the size of the sail (perhaps to fit it within the margin of his paper), and reducing the number of paddlers while increasing their size in disproportion to the length of the hull.

More errors were added back in England when the drawing was copied by an engraver on a metal plate in preparation for printing it in the official book of the voyage.

In my painting I've corrected the mistakes made in the depiction of the canoe. What you see is the work of two artists separated by two centuries.

But what of the figures? Nothing certain is known about the gourd masks, crested with ferns and bearded by tapa streamers, except that they were seen and recorded by Webber in several drawings. Anthropologists believe they had some religious significance; but then everything in the old culture had religious significance. The men may be of a priesthood, for the man on the center deck is carrying a feather image, and a sacrificial pig has been killed and set behind him.

They have set a course for Hikiau at the western end of the bay, where the rock platform of the *heiau* (temple) still stands above the beach. The yellow-dyed *tapa* capes proclaim the men as persons of status.

Webber drew during the makahiki, the season when warfare, or politics, or any work done under the patronage of the god Ku was held in abeyance. One might conclude that in the time of Lono, the priests of Ku must be masked.

Collection of Leo and Lee Chamberlain

Herb Kawainui Kane

Felice Adventurer BEARING INTO KAWAIHAE BAY, HAWAI'I
Captain John Meares wrote: *"The haziness of the morning did not obscure the varied landscape before us. The great mountain, or Mouna Kaah* [Mauna Kea], *which is situated on the North East part of the island, was clothed in clouds, which seemed, as it were, to be rolling down its declivity; while its summit towered above the vapours, and presented a sublime object of nature."*

As he neared the shore, more became visible:

"From its base to the sea was a beautiful amphitheater of villages and plantations, while the shore was crowded with people, who, from the coolness of the morning, were clothed in their parti-coloured garments. Some were seated on the banks to look at the ship, while others were running along the shore towards the little sandy patches where their canoes were drawn up, in order to come off to us.

"We hove to in the entrance of Toeyah-yah [Kawaihae] *Bay which is situated on the Western side of the Island, and consequently defended from the violence of the trade winds; nor was it long before a considerable number of canoes came off to the ship, with hogs, young pigs, taro root, plantains, sugar-cane, and fowls.*

"Indeed, such was the profusion of these articles, that many of the canoes returned without being able to dispose of their cargoes."

Collection of Herbert and Signe Behring

THE PACIFIC FUR TRADE

Homeward bound, the expedition stopped in China, and there made a discovery that would profoundly influence Hawai'i's history. Earlier, some of the men had purchased furs of the sea otter from Indians exploring the northwest coast of North America. Some were sold to Russian traders at Kamchatka; but in China, as James King wrote, "*We sold the remainder of our furs to much greater advantage—the Chinese being very Eager to purchase them and gave us from 50 to 70 dollars a skin.*" One sailor made 800 Spanish dollars, a fortune in those days.

"*The rage with which our seamen were possessed to return to Cook's River* [where furs had been bought] *and by, another cargo of skins, to make their fortunes, was not far short of mutiny.*" Two of the men deserted with the *Resolution*'s largest cutter and were never seen again.

The Spanish had known of this market, and had been sailing across the North Pacific for two hundred years before Cook's arrival, but it had not caught their interest. By treaty with Portugal, their trading sphere extended only as far west as Manila; moreover, the unpredictable temper of the Northwest Coast Indians made it a risky business. For them it was far easier to obtain gold and silver by mining it with slave labor in Mexico. Russians had been getting furs in the Aleutian Islands and Alaska long before Cook arrived there, but these the Chinese would accept only on their northern frontier, and at a much lower price than was paid in the major Chinese trading port of Canton. To British trading monopolies with stations in Canton, the idea of a pan-Pacific fur trade looked like a golden opportunity. And now they knew of islands in the mid-Pacific where provisions might be had for a few nails.

With the publication of the charts and the official account of the Cook expedition, voyages were launched from London and British India. After the close of the American Revolution the "Boston Men" jumped in. Unfettered by the chartered monopolies that restricted British traders, the self-directed Americans soon took over most of the business.

With a load of hatchets, muskets, chisels, cloth, trinkets, and other trade goods, an enterprising adventurer might sail to the Pacific, first stopping at the newly discovered Sandwich Islands for provisions and water, then continuing on to "Northwest America" to trade for furs. If he could not obtain enough furs in one summer, he might return to the islands for the winter, then head back to the coast for another summer

of trading. With a full cargo, he would then head for China, stopping again in the islands for provisions. After selling the furs, some of the profits could be invested in a cargo of tea, silk, porcelain, or other Chinese goods, and a man could sail home with his fortune made.

It was a trade which attracted rough, hardy men willing to risk all, adventurers who would face any hazard and let no Christian principle stand in the way of their making a profit. Many would not overlook a bit of piracy if it came their way. Their ships were often tiny sloops and schooners, some of which disappeared into the vast Pacific. There were deaths from scurvy at sea, from battles with Indians on land. Ships and goods might be confiscated by Spanish authorities who viewed the presence of other Europeans on the Northwest Coast, especially the British, as a challenge to Spanish claims.

Two of Cook's alumni, Nathaniel Portlock and George Dixon, sailed from England in August, 1785, and arrived at Hawai'i nine months later. After provisioning, they left for the Northwest Coast. At the same time a French expedition under La Perouse happened to be anchored off Maui. These may have been the first European ships in these waters after the Cook expedition; but the British passed by the French at night, and neither group sighted the other.

After a discouraging trading season Portlock and Dixon returned from Alaska to winter in the islands. Another expedition of two ships under John Meares and William Tipping arrived in Alaska with the idea of wintering there. Their ships were soon frozen fast in the ice.

Nearby Indians were hostile. Food and fuel ran short. As the men died of scurvy their corpses were dragged away and dropped into cracks in the ice. In May, Portlock and Dixon found Meares and Tipping still icebound with most of their men dead.

Meares asked Portlock for help, but was given it only on the condition that he get out of the fur trade and stay out. It was a deal Meares could not refuse, but not one he would honor.

He provisioned at Kauai. With the chief Kaiana as passenger, he sailed to China where he sold what furs he had. Tipping left Alaska and

FOLLOWERS OF THE EAGLE
Left: British and American traders purchased sea otter furs from Indians of the Northwest Coast.

SEA BATTLE AT MOKUOHAI
Above: During the Battle of Mokuohai between Kamehameha and his cousin Kiwalao, the rival canoe fleets fought a sea battle offshore. Weaponry used in such battles included javelins, clubs, daggers, and cutting weapons edged with shark teeth. The canoe breaker at left, a rock harnessed to a stout line, was whirled overhead and slung with great force against the hull of an enemy's canoe.
Collection of the National Geographic Society

disappeared. His ship was never seen again.

Meares found new investors and was back in 1788 with two vessels, *Felice Adventurer* and *Iphigenia Nubiana*. In his crew were Chinese sailors and shipbuilders who built the first European-style vessel ever built on the Northwest Coast, the schooner *Northwest America*. After a good trading season, Meares sailed for China in the *Felice*, leaving the others to fill their cargoes and follow. He was off Kawaihae, Hawai'i, by nightfall on October 17, 1788; and approached the shore before sunrise the next morning.

The young chief Kaiana, 6 feet 5 inches tall and of "Herculean appearance," had cut an impressive figure in China in his feather cape and helmet. A Maui chief who had been with Kahekili in the conquest of Oahu, he had later fled to Kauai after losing favor as the result of a political intrigue. Now, with an impressive quantity of Chinese goods and ironware, he landed on Hawai'i, where Kamehameha received him into his court.

To Cook's men Kamehameha had been an impetuous and fierce-looking nephew of King Kalaniopu'u, but he now ruled the northern and western districts of Hawai'i island. After Kalaniopu'u's death in 1782, his successor, Kiwalao, had viewed Kamehameha as a threat and lured him into battle, hoping to destroy him before he could gain more power. But in the battle of Mokuohai Kiwalao was killed. Now three chiefs contended for the rule of Hawai'i: Keoua of the southern district, Keawemauhili of the eastern district, and Kamehameha.

THE HAWAIIAN ARMS RACE

If Captain Cook fixed the Hawaiian Islands on the charts, it remained for the Pacific fur trade, beginning six years after his death, to open them to world attention. The sandalwood trade came later, and whalers and missionaries still later. More than any other influences in the forty years following Cook's discovery, the events of the fur trade set the course of Hawaiian history.

By 1787, Hawaiian chiefs were already in the provisioning business. Seven ships arrived that year, and the numbers increased rapidly thereafter. Iron nails quickly lost their attraction; the most valued currency soon became firearms and gunpowder. When a ruling chief acquired these, it became a matter of survival that neighboring chiefs obtain them also. Ship captains who did not offer firearms found themselves in less favorable bargaining positions than those who did.

Despite his charisma, it is doubtful that the young upstart Kamehameha could have survived the 1780s had he not controlled the best trading ports of the island of Hawai'i—sheltered bays on the leeward side of the island. Those adversaries who could not offer reasonably safe anchorages could not amass the firepower available to him. Honolulu's natural harbor could not be seen from offshore and was not known to foreigners until 1794. And while some chiefs were quick to seize by force what they could not get by trade, Kamehameha's friendly and business-like attitude toward foreigners won him a good reputation among ship captains.

SPEAKING ABOUT THE UNSPEAKABLE

Firearms made battles more deadly, but the introduction of foreign diseases was by far the greatest killer. An appalling population collapse had begun. Tuberculosis, which at this time was wiping out a third of London, was far more devastating in Hawai'i. Venereal diseases caused infertility to many of those not killed. Where the Cook expedition had met with high populations of healthy, vigorous people, the Vancouver expedition thirteen years later would find far fewer, and missionaries arriving forty two years later would find a people demoralized and dispirited.

Lieutenant King, with Cook, guessed the 1778 population at 400,000, a figure reduced by later estimates to 300,000. But King saw only the leeward coasts of islands—safer anchorages than the windward coasts, but less populated than the well-watered windward districts and fertile interiors. And King incorrectly assumed that there were no inland settlements. Now a multi-disciplined study by historian David Stannard, *Before the Horror,* has raised the estimated 1778 population to at least 800,000. A century later it had fallen to 40,000—a staggering 95% depopulation similar to those suffered in other Pacific islands as well as throughout the Americas. (Notes: 19)

KAMEHAMEHA ABOARD *FAIR AMERICAN*
Approaching Maui with his war fleet, Kamehameha converses with his English lieutenants, Isaac Davis and John Young.
Colection of Mr. and Mrs. Richard Cox

FAIR AMERICAN

THE ATTACK ON THE *FAIR AMERICAN* *Collection of Kona Village Resort*

THE "FAIR AMERICAN"

One of the first Americans to enter the fur trade was Simon Metcalfe, a veteran of the American Revolution. His ship,the *Eleanora,* mounted 10 cannon and carried a crew of 10 Europeans and 45 Chinese. With *the Eleanora* was the tiny 54' schooner *Fair American,* skippered by Metcalfe's son Thomas, 19, with a crew of four.

The two ships became separated in a stormy crossing from China to the Northwest Coast. *Fair American* arrived with severe damage and starving men, only to be captured at Nootka Sound by a Spanish squadron which had been sent north from California to enforce Spain's territorial claims against the intrusion of British traders. *Eleanora* appeared just as the Spanish were heading south with their prize, but Simon Metcalfe saw what had happened and turned away. He headed for Hawai'i, hoping that his son might get away and rejoin him at Kealakekua Bay, their rendezvous if separated.

In California, the Spanish released the *Fair American* and helped make repairs. The U.S. was, they reasoned, a friendly nation which had just survived a war with Spain's arch-enemy, Britain, and which apparently posed no threat to Spanish territorial claims. Soon young Thomas was sailing for Hawai'i to rejoin his father.

The elder Metcalfe arrived at Maui and began trading iron for provisions. Friction developed; Metcalfe may have been reluctant to deliver the agreed price for what he received. One night a boat was cut loose from the ship and the watchman asleep in it was killed. Furious, Metcalfe vowed: "If they want iron, I'll give it to them!"

Informed, if not misinformed, that the attack had come from the village of Olowalu, he sailed there. When a large number of canoes came out to trade, he gathered them all on one side of his ship, then opened fire with muskets, swivel guns, and with cannon loaded with grapeshot. More than one hundred were killed in what became known as the Olowalu Massacre.

Metcalfe proceeded to Hawai'i, where in yet another trading dispute he struck the high chief Kame'eiamoku with a rope's end and had him put off the ship. Then he coasted south to Kealakekua Bay.

Eager to improve his provisioning business, Kamehameha had ordered his chiefs not to molest foreigners; but it was Metcalfe's ill luck to have struck a chief who by rank and seniority could ignore that order. Kamanawa and Kame'eiamoku were the twin brothers who had been Kamehameha's protectors since his birth. Now Kame'eiamoku had been struck by a foreigner before his people, an outrage to his honor which demanded vengeance. He vowed to capture the next foreign ship that came by.

That happened to be *Fair American.* Without knowing that its captain was the son of the man who had struck him Kame'eiamoku attacked, heaving Thomas Metcalfe into the sea where he was killed. Then the sailors were killed, all except the mate, Isaac Davis, temporarily blinded and badly wounded but spared by Kame'eiamoku because of the fierce courage he displayed in battle.

When word of the attack reached Kamehameha at Kealakekua Bay, he prohibited any contact with the *Eleanora* to prevent Metcalfe from hearing about it. John Young, Metcalfe's boatswain, happened to be on shore, and was not permitted to return to the ship. Wondering why no canoes would approach his ship, Metcalfe waited for several days with growing impatience and alarm, then sent a letter ashore to the three European sailors residing there. Threatening to cannonade the village if Young were not returned, he promised "*... consequences of an unpleasant nature ... I am possessed of sufficient powers to take ample revenge, which it is your duty to make the head chief acquainted with.*"

He fired signal guns for several more days, but received no communication. Reluctant to venture ashore himself, he eventually sailed away. Killed in a dispute with Northwest Coast Indians some time later, he never learned that by his own behavior he had caused his son's death.

Kamehameha had little tolerance for foreign seamen, most of whom proved lazy and troublesome; but Young, 41, and Davis, 33, were officers with expertise he needed. Promising them good treatment, he set them to work training his men to use muskets, sail the *Fair American*, and serve its swivel guns and four-pounder cannon.

Young was soon nicknamed "Olohana" because of his habit of shouting "all hands!" during training, and later as a rallying cry in battle. A cannon on *Fair American* was affectionately named Robert, which Hawaiians pronounced "Lopaka". It was probably no more than a four pounder, but it took a well-drilled crew to serve and fire it with maximum rapidity during a battle. It was also used on land, mounted on a wheeled carriage. When Kamehameha invaded Maui a few months later, the Maui force was pressed into the narrow Iao Valley. Here cannonfire cut swaths in the Maui ranks, creating such terror and confusion that they lost heart and were routed.

Kamehameha next invaded Molokai, but was forced to abandon his campaign when news came that his adversary in southern Hawai'i, Keoua Kuahu'ula, had launched a major campaign against him. He returned to Hawai'i and fought Keoua to a stalemate.

In one battle a cannon was lost when Keoua's men bravely charged as it was being reloaded. Young and Davis ran for their lives and narrowly escaped.

Spurred by the news that Kamehameha was building a great war temple which, if completed, might bring him the full power of his war god, the ruling chiefs of Maui, Oahu, and Kauai launched a fleet of war canoes against his Hawai'i homeland. They struck at the rich valleys of Waipi'o and Waimanu. Kamehameha sailed there, mustering canoes and men along the Kohala coast. After a desperate sea battle, the invading fleet was put to flight.

The action became known as Kepuwahaulaula (the red-mouthed gun). Both sides had firearms and the help of a few foreigners. Swivel-guns were mounted on the bows of some double canoes. But Kamehameha also had *Fair American* and its cannon. Without this little schooner, he might well have lost the day, and his life, in the rough, shark-filled waters off Waimanu Valley. And without a chief who could bring the islands under one rule, the subsequent history of these islands would have been radically altered.

Young and Davis became loyal subjects of Kamehameha, serving him as trustworthy lieutenants in his conquests and in his commerce with foreign ships. They received lands and honors, married into chiefly families, and remained in the islands for the rest of their lives.

AFTERWORD

In November, 1983, my painting of *Fair American* in action in the Battle of the Red-mouthed Gun was published in a *National Geographic* article about Kamehameha. Soon afterward a letter came from a Mr. Henry Despard in Michigan. He identified himself as a descendant of Simon Metcalfe, and asked technical questions about my depiction of the ship. I replied by mail, and he telephoned to thank me. He had been doing research on his ancestor, and in our chat he mentioned that there were two branches of Metcalfe's descendants, but they had lost touch with each other long ago.

A week later another letter arrived, but this was from an Edward Metcalfe in New Jersey. He asked much the same questions about *Fair American*, and as proof of his lineage enclosed a photocopy of Metcalfe's last letter home. Posted from Macao in 1789, the letter described a fierce gun battle with Chinese pirates in which two officers and a number of the *Eleanora* crew were killed. Edward Metcalfe was interested in his family's history, but seemed to be unaware of Mr. Despard's research. On an impulse, I enclosed a copy of Despard's letter along with my reply—and sent off a copy of Edward Metcalfe's letter to Henry Despard.

Several days later Mr. Despard telephoned:

"Mr. Kane, I want to thank you. I've just been on the telephone for two hours with a cousin in New Jersey whose existence has been unknown to me. We're planning to hold a family reunion, and you're invited."

I was unable to accept, but promised that if he ever came to Hawai'i I would be pleased to introduce him to a friend who is descended from Kame'eiamoku, the chief who killed his great uncle Thomas 193 years earlier.

THE BATTLE OF THE RED-MOUTHED GUN
Collection of the Army Museum, Fort De Russy, Honolulu
Reproduced by permission of The National Geographic Society.

FAIR AMERI
H Kawainui Kane

THE BUILDING OF PU'UKOHOLA

THE ARRIVAL OF KEOUA BELOW PU'UKOHOLA

THE POWER OF A TEMPLE

Kamehameha decided to build a great *heiau* (temple) at Kawaihae to his war god, Ku-kaili-moku, by which the help of that god might be invoked. A priest-architect shaped an earthen model of it, and the call went out.

Thousands of men passed rocks from hand to hand over great distances. Stoneworkers fitted the rocks without mortar. Kamehameha himself led the work, raising rock platforms and walls.

News of the temple-building would have been received with dismay by the kings of the other islands, and may have caused them to rush to attack Hawai'i without adequate preparation, hoping to crush Kamehameha before he could complete the temple. If so, the building of Pu'ukohola (hill of the whale), was a masterstroke of psychological warfare.

When Pu'ukohola was completed, Kamehameha sent emissaries to his rival for the rule of Hawai'i Island, Keoua Kuahu'ula, inviting him to parley. Keoua, shaken by the loss of a third of his army in a volcanic eruption, and believing that the goddess Pele had turned against him, accepted. Heedless of the warnings of others, Keoua sailed with his fleet. He stopped at Kiholo Bay to perform rites of purification, asking those who would accompany him in his canoe to bring no weapons and to prepare themselves to be his companions in death.

When the fleet reached its destination, Kamehameha was waiting on the beach with a crowd of his men. Walking out into the water, Kamehameha called to Keoua to come ashore. But as Keoua stepped out of his canoe, the impetuous Kona chief Ke'eaumoku, in sudden fury, leaped forward and threw a spear. Before Kamehameha could stop the fighting that followed, Keoua and all but one of the warriors in his canoe were killed.

The corpses were offered to the god in the consecration of the temple. Kamehameha was now the king of all Hawai'i Island. But whether he had planned to kill his rival, or had intended to discuss peace, we will never know. (Notes: 20)

A CEREMONY AT PU'UKOHOLA HEIAU (ABOVE)
All paintings: National Park Service Collection

H.M.A.T. *BOUNTY* OFF TAHITI, 1788
Lieutenant William Bligh, Captain of His Majesty's Armed Transport *Bounty*, had, at age 24, served as Captain Cook's sailing master. Nine years later he returned to the Pacific on a mission to transport breadfruit plants to the West Indies, where it might be grown as food for plantation slaves.

The Polynesian breadfruit tree does not produce viable seeds, but must be propagated by transplanting young plants which sprout from the roots of a mature tree.

Bounty was only 91 feet long, and the ship's company of 46 was further crowded by a large space designed for carrying the plants. After enduring weeks of gales and heavy seas in an unsuccessful attempt to get into the Pacific by rounding Cape Horn, Bligh turned his battered ship downwind and ran for the Pacific across the South Atlantic and the Indian Ocean, arriving in Tahiti after a ten month voyage with his men surly over the bad food and Bligh's frequent ill temper.

In the painting, *Bounty* coasts off Tahiti, passing a Tahitian sailing canoe headed the other way. The painting is based on the original plans for the ship, now in the National Maritime Museum, Greenwich, England.

Collection of Edward and Lynn Hogan

SERVING A CANNON ABOARD BOUNTY
Collection of Charles Porter

THE *BOUNTY* AT TUBUAI

MOST of the western world's literate population has read *Mutiny on the Bounty*, and the other books of *The Bounty Trilogy* by Charles Nordhoff and James Norman Hall. It is probable that those who have not read the books have at least seen one of the movies based on *Mutiny on the Bounty*, the world's best known sea story.

It is generally believed that after the mutineers threw Captain Bligh off the *Bounty* they returned to Tahiti, picked up some Tahitians, and headed for safe haven at uninhabited Pitcairn's Island. Nordhoff and Hall gave one chapter scant attention, and consequently it was omitted by the movies as well—the story of Christian's effort to establish a settlement on the island of Tubuai in the Austral Islands four hundred miles south of Tahiti.

Nordhoff and Hall abbreviated the Tubuai story because they lacked solid information. The one full account, the journal of gunner James Morrison, had disappeared until recently.

Bligh's mission was to gather breadfruit sprouts in Tahiti and transport them to the British West Indies, where the trees might produce food for plantation slaves. His men, most of them very young, found in Tahiti a lifestyle far more appealing, and girls more bewitching, than any they had known. Their reluctance to leave, exacerbated by Bligh's harshness, brought about a mutiny led by Fletcher Christian on April 28, 1789, when the ship was a month out of Tahiti.

Off Tonga, Bligh was put over the side along with as many loyalists as the longboat would hold. He escaped almost certain death by an amazing voyage to the Dutch East Indies. Upon his return to England, the *Pandora* was dispatched under Captain Edward Edwards to search for the mutineers.

Morrison, unable to find room in Bligh's boat, was forced to remain on *Bounty*. Bligh wrongfully listed him as a mutineer.

BOUNTY

BOUNTY ENTERING MATAVAI BAY, TAHITI

Left: Led by a boat taking soundings, *Bounty* is surrounded by the canoes of curious Tahitians. A light puff in the early morning calm fills the sails for a moment as the ship ghosts into the bay. Taking no chances on the reception, Bligh has ordered swivel guns mounted.

Tahiti had come to Britain's attention only twenty one years earlier. With its naturally abundant environment, comfortable climate, and charming people—especially its amorous women—it was a paradise to European sailors by comparison with their life at sea and the harsh existence most had known in England. After a stay of almost six months, most of the men had formed relationships with Tahitian women, and many were reluctant to leave.

With a thousand breadfruit plants loaded aboard, Bligh rounded up his crew, flogged those who had attempted to desert, and departed.

Collection of Nick and Nancy Rutgers

BLIGH'S SURVIVAL VOYAGE AFTER THE MUTINY

Above right: After departing from Tahiti, long-suppressed anger burst into mutiny. Bligh and 18 loyalists were put into a 23 foot launch with some rations and water, and cut adrift.

A search for food at nearby Tonga ended in a frightening escape in which one man was killed by natives. Bligh resolved to try to reach the nearest European settlement, Timor, in the Dutch East Indies, 3,600 miles to the west. He now proved himself as a master seaman and a resolute leader.

The voyage took 47 days, much of it in heavy weather. Bligh did much of the steering himself, for any mistake at the tiller could cause a fatal swamping or capsize. The boat was so overloaded that there were only eight inches of freeboard. In constant danger of being swamped by following seas, the crew kept it afloat only by continuous bailing.

Passing through the Fiji Islands, they narrowly escaped pursuing canoes. Off the Australian coast they found hazardous reefs and hostile natives.

Spoiled bread and meat were rationed to several ounces per day. A few birds were caught by hand, and shellfish were found on small deserted islands. Close to death, their emaciated bodies covered with sores and sunburn, they made it to the Dutch settlement at Timor.

One man died there, and several more caught a fever and died at Batavia. Bligh and eleven others reached England.

The painting follows Bligh's description in his journal at dawn after running in heavy weather throughout a stormy night.

Private Collection

TUBUAI

Immediately after the mutiny Christian sailed for Tubuai. Captain Cook had sighted the island and charted its position, but had not landed. An island about three by five miles in size, Tubuai is surrounded by a broad lagoon enclosed by a fringing coral reef.

As *Bounty* entered the only passage through the reef, it was attacked by men in a large canoe armed with spears. The assault was beaten off with pistol fire.

On the following day a large double canoe put out from shore carrying eighteen *"weomen neatly dressed and their heads and necks decorated with flowers and pearl shells, as they approached the ship they stood up and beat time to a song... they were all young and handsom having fine long hair which reached their Waists in waving ringlets. They came on board without ceremony..."*

But the *Bounty* men were not too distracted to notice about fifty canoes filled with men, some blowing conch shells, approaching on the other side. When the men showed their weapons, the girls were put off the ship, and cannon were fired into the massed war canoes to discourage the attack. Shocked by their first experience with cannon, the Tubuaians headed for the beach. When the British manned their boats and followed them, they were met by a hail of rocks. Muskets were fired, and the natives disappeared into the brush. The next day the British went ashore. They were favorably impressed with the island as a hideaway, but could make no contact with the natives.

Undaunted, Christian returned to Tahiti to provision the ship and enlist some Tahitians. The Bounty was back at Tubuai a month later loaded with livestock and plants with which to start a new settlement.

This time the reception was cordial. Christian made a friendship pact with the chief of the largest of the three districts—a friendship lost when he decided to build the settlement in another district—one which offered concealment from a ship entering the pass. Work began on a fort, named Fort George in honor of the king against whom they had mutinied—a square of 100 yards with sod walls and a moat around it. *Bounty* was laboriously hauled against the prevailing wind from "Bloody Bay", the scene of the first attack, through several miles of the shallow lagoon studded with coral heads to an anchorage just offshore of the fort. The ship was kedged by hauling anchors ahead of it, then winching the ship forward. The work of dismantling began at its final anchorage off the site of the fort.

Provisioning excursions to other districts came under attack. The mutineers' greatest complaint, however, was neither the brutal work nor the danger, but the lack of women. They had not brought enough women from Tahiti, and the girls of their chosen district were friendly but not sexually cooperative. In September, when Christian put the matter to a vote, it was decided to return to Tahiti.

The end came when the British and their Tahitian allies tried to round up straying livestock and got into a battle with the Tubuaians of neighboring districts. Under repeated assaults they retreated to the fort, keeping up a defensive fire with their muskets. Their firearms saved them from annihilation; they suffered four wounded but remarkably lost not a man.

BOUNTY AT "BLOODY BAY"
As the decoy girls are put off the ship, an attack by massed war canoes is averted by cannon fire—a sudden explosion to which some of the warriors at this instant have not yet reacted. It is their first contact with Europeans.
Few artifacts of the original Tubuai culture still exist, but Morrison's descriptions, corroborated and augmented by materials from other islands in the Australs, enabled me to depict the canoes, dress, and weapons with some measure of confidence. With a borrowed fishing canoe, I was able to study the island from *Bounty's* anchorage.
Artist's Collection. Copyright

MORRISON'S BAD LUCK

Back in Tahiti they split up. Some stayed in Tahiti when Christian sailed off on the long search for a hideaway which ended at Pitcairn's Island. When the *Pandora* arrived searching for the mutineers Morrison paddled a canoe out to meet it but was clapped in irons—Captain Edwards refused to believe that he was not one of the mutineers. All who were captured were cruelly treated regardless of guilt or innocence, and kept chained in an airless box on deck. Several

BOUNTY

drowned when *Pandora* struck the Australian barrier reef and went down, a death which Morrison narrowly escaped. The survivors suffered greatly during a replay of Bligh's longboat voyage to the East Indies.

In England Morrison was sentenced to death, but no evidence could be brought that he had taken part in the mutiny, and since he had voluntarily surrendered at Tahiti, he was saved by the King's pardon.

Morrison returned to the Navy. Some years later Admiral Sir Thomas Troubridge chose Morrison to serve as master gunner on his flagship, *Blenheim*, on the East India Station. When the aging *Blenheim* was pronounced unfit for further sea duty, Troubridge sailed her for Capetown despite warnings that she would become the coffin of all on board. *Blenheim* left Madras in 1807 and was never seen again. The ship and all aboard were presumed to have gone down in a gale off Madagascar.

One captain tried to hang James Morrison. Another nearly drowned him—a death ultimately accomplished by the recklessness of still a third.

JAMES MORRISON, ETHNOGRAPHER

While in jail awaiting trial Morrison had written a lengthy narrative of his *Bounty* adventure, replete with detailed observations on the islanders' customs, society, material culture and mode of life. Morrison was a born ethnographer. What little is known of the original culture of Tubuai is glimpsed through his descriptive writings. After the Bounty episode Tubuai was visited by traders who wrote nothing of their observations, and much of the culture was surely lost when the population was ravaged by epidemics of European diseases. When English missionaries arrived they were more interested in making converts than in recording what they saw. Later, under French rule, immigration from Tahiti turned Tubuai into a Tahitian cultural province. The distinctive original culture as well as most of its objects have largely disappeared.

Morrison had left his journal with another *Bounty* survivor, Peter Heywood, when he returned to sea. It vanished around 1870, but was found six decades later at the Mitchell Library, Sydney, to which it had been bequeathed by an immigrant to Australia. (Notes: 21)

While doing research for paintings of the *Bounty* at Tubuai, a work funded by the National Geographic Society, I found that some of Morrison's descriptions of Tubuaian objects which no longer exist could be verified and augmented by the cultural records and artifacts of other islands in the Austral group. For example, his description of the intricate carving of a Tubuai spear is perfectly matched by a spear from nearby Rurutu in the Tahiti Museum. Also, his description of curious beehive-shaped battle helmets is matched by early photographs of such helmets worn by warriors in Atiu.

The research trip to Tahiti and Tubuai was greatly assisted by James Norman Hall's daughter and son-in-law, Nancy and Nick Rutgers of Hawai'i and Tahiti, and made in the pleasant company of *National Geographic* writer Luis Marden and photographer Robert Caputo. Nick

BUILDING FORT GEORGE

"... we proceeded to Work tho not a man knew anything of Fortification; some Cut stakes others made Battins some Cut Sods & brought to hand, some built and others Wrought in the ditch, the Carpenters made barrows & Cut timber for the Gates and Drawbridge, & the work began to rise apace. Nor was Mr. Christian an Idle Spectator for He always took a part in the Most Laborious part of the Work, and half a Pint of Porter was served twice a day extra."

is a leading authority on the *Bounty* events, and with Luis had cleared the site of the fort years earlier in order to photograph it.

The only difficulty was that someone on Tubuai had dreamed that gold was buried at the fort site. When we arrived, several men were at work on an excavation ten feet deep, and our interest in the site aroused a suspicion that we were actually there for the gold. Such fears were allayed by Nancy, who was taken at her word because she has relatives on Tubuai. The land at the site is sandy. The walls of the fort are now reduced to a low berm, and the moat has become a shallow swale. The depth of water in the excavation actually enabled me to determine the water level in the moat for my painting of the building of Fort George.

What may be the one surviving unique feature of the old culture in Tubuai is the local preference for rigging the float of an outrigger canoe on the right side, whereas throughout Polynesia the float is mounted off the left. When I asked a canoemaker for an explanation, he could only say that it had always been done this way.

WHY I DELETED THE 'FLAG LOCKER'

After a painting is done for *National Geographic*, researchers are assigned to question the accuracy of every detail. This is no hardship for the artist who can justify his decisions, the exception being one who lives in Hawai'i and receives 3 AM phone calls from researchers in Washington, D.C. who have forgotten the time difference.

One question about my painting of the *Bounty* at Tubuai was the absence of the "flag locker." The researcher informed me that a new book about the *Bounty* had been published in England, a definitive work which included all existing information about the ship. The author had made numerous drawings, and every view of the deck showed a curious vertical structure at the stern rail described in captions as the flag locker. Why, asked the researcher, had I omitted it from my depiction of *Bounty*? (Notes: 22)

I explained that it was not a flag locker. The Pacific was hardly the place where flag signals with other ships would be expected, so there would be no reason for a flag locker of such size to take up space on *Bounty's* tiny quarterdeck. At the National Maritime Museum, Greenwich, England, while studying the original construction drawings for conversion of the *Bethia* into the *Bounty*, I had called the attention of the Curator of Draughts to this structure overhanging the stern, and had been informed that Bligh had ordered it built as his private privy.

The researcher was not amused. But he did make a call to Greenwich, and later called me back to say that he would allow that it may have been a privy. Now the question was, why did I omit it from my painting?

I confessed that it had been a judgment on my part. After Bligh had been tossed overboard, the baleful presence of his private privy on *Bounty's* cramped quarterdeck would have caused that to be tossed overboard as well.

THE CANOE OF TEHANI'S FAMILY
Left: The Tahitian double canoe described by Nordhoff and Hall in *Mutiny on the Bounty*
Collection of Mr. and Mrs. Alfred Kwiecinski

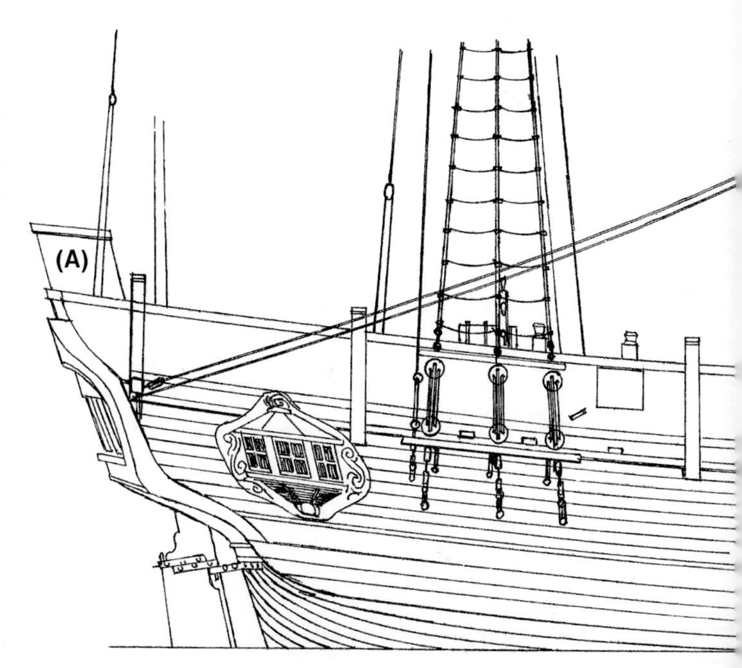

The curious structure at the stern ("A" at right)

Captain Vancouver and the Case of the Insubordinate Midshipman

A well-deserved spanking may have kept Hawai'i out of the British Empire, and changed the course of Pacific history.

SAILING HOME in 1795, George Vancouver had earned a hero's welcome. A diplomatic mission to Spanish California had secured British commerce in the Pacific. The treaty he had worked out with Kamehameha would bring Hawai'i into the empire, giving British ships a safe and dependable source of provisions in the mid-Pacific. He had added more than 200 discoveries to the map of Australia and the Pacific Ocean. In all, his achievements in the north Pacific had far exceeded those of his mentor, Captain James Cook. And for good measure, he had captured a Dutch ship on the way home.

What awaited him, however, was not glory, but a public furor that would destroy his career and hasten an early death at the age of forty.

It had been a wearing, dangerous voyage of more than four years. The largest ship in his tiny squadron, *Discovery*, was only 99 feet long, uncomfortably cramped with 100 men and the supplies necessary for a voyage around the world. His ships had been wracked by storms and shoals. But discipline among the crew had been preserved, and with the loss of only one man a new health record had been set. Vancouver's own health, however, was failing, at 37, after a total of twenty two years of service at sea.

Back in England, his achievements were overshadowed by controversy over punishment he had allegedly dealt to a young midshipman (officer-cadet) during the voyage. There were class distinctions separating lower ranks (commoners) from officers (gentlemen). A captain could order a commoner flogged for a paltry offence; but strike a gentleman, and one could expect a challenge to a duel with him or any member of his family. Midshipmen, who often went to sea as boys, were regarded as "the young gentlemen" and were exempt from flogging.

But what made the charge newsworthy was that the midshipman, Thomas Pitt, was a member of one of the most influential families in England and a cousin of the Prime Minister, "Pitt the Younger."

By all accounts, Thomas Pitt was a lad of impulsive and wanton behavior, possessed by an ungovernable temper. On the voyage he had become so troublesome that Vancouver had put him ashore at Hawai'i. Pitt found passage on a trading ship and reached home. His father had died, and he was now Lord Camelford. He brought charges against Vancouver. The case became a sensation, and the press feasted on it.

HMS *DISCOVERY*
Not to be confused with Cook's *Discovery*, this ship was built on the Thames in 1789 and fitted out for a long voyage of exploration. *Discovery* was 99 feet in hull length with a burden of 337 tons. Bronze or copper fastened, her bottom copper-sheathed, the ship mounted ten four-pounders and ten swivel guns. After the voyage she was refitted as a bomb vessel, and served in the wars with France. She was made into a prison hulk in 1808, and broken up in 1834.

Painting commissioned by Nick G. Maggos; presently in the Collection of Ariana A. Fairbanks

Camelford challenged Vancouver to a duel. Vancouver had retired to his brothers house in the country to prepare his journal of the voyage for publication. Ill with what may have been tuberculosis, he responded by stating that any unpleasantness his lordship had experienced on the voyage had been brought upon himself by his lordship's own behavior, and had been necessary for the preservation of the ship's discipline. He then accepted the duel on the condition that all the evidence be presented to any admiral of the Navy, who would then determine whether or not he was liable, by the laws of honor, to be called upon. If such guilt were found, Vancouver declared, he would very cheerfully give his lordship full satisfaction on the field of honor.

It was the proper response, but Camelford rejected the condition. At a chance meeting on a London street, Camelford flew into a rage and beat Vancouver with his walking stick until restrained by passers-by. Further persecution at last brought a writ of restraint from the Lord Chancellor, ordering Camelford to put up a large sum as a bond.

Shortly after Vancouver's death in 1798, Camelford was court-martialed on the charge of murdering a fellow officer, but was acquitted in spite of strong evidence. Thereafter the Navy repeatedly passed him over for promotion until he took the hint and resigned. Later, he challenged a friend over a rumored insult and got himself killed.

Historians have suggested that the treaty which would have brought Hawai'i into the empire fell into a bureaucratic crack and disappeared because of Parliament's preoccupation with European problems. But perhaps it was deliberately nudged into obscurity, as was Vancouver, for during all the fuss about the flogging, what politician would dare risk his career by introducing the treaty to Parliament and facing the wrath of the Pitt family? An incident as trivial as the spanking of Thomas Pitt may have had far-reaching consequences, changing the course of history throughout the Pacific.

A *PELELEU* WAR CANOE
The *peleleu* were a class of large war canoes developed by Kamehameha's designers for his conquest of the islands. More than 800 were built on Hawai'i, the hulls carved from gigantic koa trees. Sails were cut in the European mode, but made of traditional plaited *lauhala* (pandanus leaf) matting. Some were decked over completely at the stern to increase their cargo capacity.

In what may be the first detailed painting of a *peleleu* canoe, an average length of 70' is depicted. A swivel gun is mounted in the bows.
Collection of Cathy Bechtel Reed

WHAT IF HAWAI'I HAD BECOME BRITISH?

First the name Hawai'i would now apply only to the largest island in the archipelago. These would still be the Sandwich Islands, as Cook had named them. Kamehameha's conquests would have brought the other islands under the rule of Hawai'i Island, but not under a government named "The Kingdom of Hawai'i."

Nor would the indigenous Polynesians know themselves as Hawaiians, but more likely as Sandwich Island Maoli, distinguishing them from the Maori of the Cook Islands and New Zealand. *Maori,* or the Hawaiian variant *maoli,* means 'native'.

If the subsequent history of these islands were similar to the history of Fiji, or other Pacific societies where the British found an authority structure and land tenure system similar to that of Hawai'i, the Sandwich Islands would today be an independent nation and a member of the Commonwealth. Chiefly power would be land-based. While Americans were eager to own land, the British were usually content to lease land for plantations. Only where a central authority structure was not found, such as in New Zealand where Maori tribes were incessantly at war, did the British wind up taking most of the land.

In Fiji only 8% of the land is "freehold" and may be bought and sold. Some 10% is owned by the government, and 82% is owned by the chiefs and people in common, managed by the chiefs acting as a native land trust board. Had Parliament accepted Vancouver's treaty, land tenure and chiefly power in the Sandwich Islands today might be very similar.

Today, throughout most of the Pacific Islands, the greater part of the lands remain under native ownership. Except in Hawaii and Guam, land either cannot be purchased by foreigners or can be acquired only under severe restrictions.

Over two centuries the history of immigration to the Sandwich Islands would have been quite different from what has actually taken place. Plantation labor from India might have been preferred to laborers from China, Japan,

Korea, or Portugal. And without the "American connection," there would have been few immigrants from the U.S, the Philippines, Puerto Rico and Samoa. Immigration from the British Isles might have included convict labor from England, contract laborers from poverty-stricken Scotland, and refugees from the Irish potato famine. The countless accidents of meetings, matings, and movings over two centuries would have been so completely different that no person living today with ancestral roots in Hawai'i would have been born.

Without a developing economic interest in Hawai'i, American interest in the Pacific might never have developed. The U.S. might not have sent its fleet to cajole Japan into opening its door to the west; and the Pacific war, insofar as it was a result of Japanese modernization and expansion, might never have happened.

HOW VANCOUVER WON THE TREATY

Britain's missed opportunity was made possible by Vancouver's extraordinary civility and diplomacy, through which he won for Britain the enduring friendship of Kamehameha and other ruling chiefs.

He had first encountered Hawaiians while serving as a midshipman under Captain Cook. Having been severely beaten in a scuffle the day before Cook was killed, he knew them as no strangers to violence. Thirteen years later he returned as captain of the second British expedition. Between 1792 and 1794 he made three visits to the Sandwich Islands, calling on chiefs of each of the "four kingdoms."

"Under a conviction of the importance of these islands to Great Britain, in the event of an extension of her commerce over the Pacific Ocean, I lost no opportunity for encouraging their friendly dispositions toward us ..."

Friendly dispositions and a peaceful Hawai'i meant safety for British ships; and though Vancouver presented himself as a benefactor by distributing cattle and seeds of new food plants, he was, in his hope of developing a dependable mid-Pacific provisioning base, attending to British interests.

Hawaiians had seen few like him. Many foreigners were troublesome: piratical sea captains who did little to conceal their disdain for the customs of their hosts; rude seamen who deserted their ships, some spreading deadly new diseases. Vancouver was outraged at the behavior of some unscrupulous traders, which he described as "... *not only infamously fraudulent but barbarous and inhuman.*"

While serving under Cook he had known Kamehameha as a fierce-looking, impetuous young chief. Now he was astonished to find Kamehameha transformed into a man of impressive dignity, geniality, and diplomacy—and as businesslike as any London merchant.

Nor had the chief lost his skills in the martial arts. Vancouver witnessed a demonstration at a military tournament in which Kamehameha ordered six blunt spears hurled simultaneously at him with full force. He caught two, parried three, and dodged one.

Vancouver's initial proposal for cession was parried by his host, who declined to consider it

KAMEHAMEHA CATCHING SPEARS
Collection of William Donnelly

H.M.S. *DISCOVERY* OFF THE PUNA COAST, HAWAI'I
Vancouver and Kamehameha sailed from Hilo to Kealakekua Bay in January 1774. The mountains Mauna Kea and Mauna Loa were both capped with snow. Observing "columns of smoke," Vancouver learned from Kamehameha that these were caused by "subterranean fires." This may have been an eruption of Kilauea volcano on the flank of Mauna Loa. The brig *Chatham* is visible in the distance.
Collection of William and Helen Larson

DISCOVERY

unless a British warship was stationed at Hawai'i to "*...assist in the defense of the island.*" While this impressed the naturalist Archibald Menzies as "*a very strong and reasonable argument,*" it also suggests that Kamehameha was seeking a treaty of protection and military alliance rather than outright cession. Vancouver could not promise this, nor would he comply with Kamehameha's persistent requests for a supply of firearms. In a final compromise he had his carpenters build Kamehameha a small schooner, the *Britannia,* providing demonstrations of shipbuilding skills that were quickly learned by Hawaiian canoe makers.

Persistent and most eager to be of service, Vancouver almost went too far. On his last visit to Hawai'i, he involved himself in one of Kamehameha's frequent domestic difficulties with the beautiful and willful Ka'ahumanu. Observing the king's despondent mood as they sailed together from Hilo around to Kealakekua Bay, Vancouver wrote:

"*I understood from the king's attendants, that the infidelity of the queen was by no means certain; and as I well knew the reciprocal affection of this royal pair, and as she was then residing with her father at, or in the neighborhood of Karakakooa* [Kealakekua], *I thought it a charitable office to make a tender of my endeavors for the purpose of bringing about a reconciliation. In reply to this obtrusion of my services, Tamaahmaah expressed his thanks; and assured me, that he should always be happy to receive my advice on state affairs, or any public matters, especially where peace or war may be concerned; but that such differences as*

Photo: Harold Yoshida

THE YOUNG KAMEHAMEHA
Left: A larger-than-life bronze sculpture interpretive of the young Kamehameha at the height of his struggle for power.
The statue was commissioned by developer Takeshi Sekiguchi, and Installed at the entrance to the The Grand Hyatt Hotel, Wailea, Maui.
Modelling assistance, moldmaking and wax castings by Alois Valenta. Foundrywork by the Hammerman Foundry.

THE BATTLE AT NU'UANU PALI
Right: Kamehameha landed a huge invasion fleet on Oahu in 1795 and skirmished with the Oahu forces as he advanced across the plain where Honolulu now stands. The Oahu army made a stand but was driven up Nu'uanu valley in hard fighting. The upper valley terminates at the brink of a thousand-foot cliff (*pali*), and here those of the Oahu army who found no escape along the ridges or down a narrow cliffside trail were driven over the precipice.
Both sides used firearms as well as traditional weapons, and included a few foreigners in their ranks. In the narrow upper valley Kamehameha's well-disciplined phalanx, a tight formation carrying long lances, could not be stopped.
Collection of Nick G. Maggos

that such differences as might occur, or respect, his domestic happiness, he considered to be totally out of my province. This rebuff I silently sustained."

At Kealakekua Bay the two devised a ruse that aptly demonstrates their friendship. Vancouver invited the queen and her party to his ship for an entertainment. On a signal, Kamehameha came aboard pretending to be unaware of Ka'ahumanu's presence. As the two stood face to face, both burst into tears; and Vancouver, taking them each by the hand, brought them together. They embraced to the applause of all present.

At the close of Vancouver's third and last visit to Hawai'i, Kamehameha called the ruling chiefs of the island to a council at Kealakekua Bay. Lengthy discussions were held; arguments for and against cession were offered, with Vancouver present to answer all questions. The matter was concluded in a formal meeting of the highest chiefs aboard *Discovery*. Kamehameha made a fine speech about the advantages of British protection. The throng on shore hailed the news with enthusiasm, and the British flag was raised with ceremony.

Largely due to Vancouver, Hawaiian chiefs developed feelings of friendship toward Britain which persisted throughout the 19th century far out of proportion to the British presence.

He was one of the most outstanding of 18th century explorers; yet his life is one of the least documented. His simple grave in England was neglected for many years until the people of Vancouver, British Columbia took charge of its perpetual care. (Notes: 23)

TAMEHAMEHA

Right: Drawings of Kamehameha by European artists were not made until his later years. This painting is an interpretation which attempts to present him twenty five years earlier, as written descriptions suggest he may have appeared in the early 1790s. He knew himself as Tamehameha, before the "T" became "K" in a language change. Kamehameha literally means "The Lonely One." Considered an upstart by rival ruling chiefs who sought to crush him, he was impelled to seek victory less by the urge for conquest than by the need for personal survival. Later he saw that his people could survive as a nation only if all the islands were consolidated under one government.

A carefully researched description of him was written by King David Kalakaua, the last Hawaiian king: *"Kamehameha was a man of tremendous physical and intellectual strength. In any land and in any age he would have been a leader. The impress of his mind remains with his crude and vigorous laws, and wherever he stepped is seen an imperishable track. He was so strong of limb that ordinary men were but children in his grasp, and in council the wisest yielded to his judgment. He seems to have been born a man and to have had no boyhood. He was always sedate and thoughtful, and from his earliest years cared for no sport or pastime that was not manly. He had a harsh and rugged face, less given to smiles than frowns, but strongly marked with lines indicative of self reliance and changeless purpose. He was barbarous, unforgiving and merciless to his enemies, but just, sagacious and considerate in dealing with his subjects. He was more feared than loved and respected; but his strength of arm and force of character well fitted him for the supreme chieftaincy of the group, and he accomplished what no one else could have done in his day."**

**His Hawaiian Majesty Kalakaua,* The Legends and Myths of Hawaii, *(1888), p. 384*

Collection of Thomas Hoey

KAMEHAMEHA AT KAMAKAHONU

Right: The wars were over and the Kingdom of Hawaii firmly established. At Kamakahonu, his estate at Kailua Village in Kona, Kamehameha devoted his last years to ruling his kingdom as a benevolent and just monarch, encouraging prosperity, conducting business with foreigners, and educating his son Liholiho as his successor. The painting depicts him wearing a simple *kapa* garment in conversation with his son Liholiho. Beside him stands his prime minister, Kalanimoku. The prince's attendant, wearing a short yellow cape, is John Papa I'i, who later became an important historian. The fish in the foreground represent the gifts of food brought daily to the court. Two ladies of the court are seated at left. Kamehameha's residence was a complex of thatched structures around a tranquil cove at Kailua Bay. Across the cove stands his private temple, 'Ahu'ena.

Collection of the King Kamehameha Hotel

THE INCIDENT OF THE SPLINTERED PADDLE

While sailing along an enemy's coastline during an early campaign, Kamehameha spotted people peacefully fishing, and leaped ashore to attack them. When his foot was caught in a lava crevice, one of the fleeing fishermen turned and broke a canoe paddle over his head.

Years later Kamehameha regretted his behavior and had the fishermen found and brought before him. They expected to be killed; some of the chiefs cried "stone them!"

But Kamehameha said "It is I who should be stoned."

He then proclaimed the Law of the Splintered Paddle, which gave commoners protection against wanton mistreatment by chiefs.

Collection of Norman MacDonald

'AHU'ENA HEIAU, 1817

In the foreground Kamehameha's business agent John Young and a visiting foreign officer are in conversation with two guards beside one of the eighteen cannon that faced the bay. The thatched building in the distance at right is the king's retreat, the doorway concealed by a small guardhouse where Kamehameha could keep watch over the traffic in the bay as well as view his upland plantations without being seen. The heiau (temple), built on a platform of rockwork, was dedicated to patron spirits of learning, the arts, and healing.

In 1975 I was pleased to receive an assignment from Mervin Gilliland, Vice President, Amfac, Inc., builder of the Hotel King Kamehameha, to design a reconstruction of the heiau based on archaeology and research done by the Bishop Museum. Accurate replication was made possible by drawings of the original structure by European visitors and contemporary descriptions by John Papa I'i, which included the materials used. The laborious work was done by Hawaiian artisans led by David Mauna Roy. The largest structure, the hale mana (house of power), required more than three hundred thousand ti leaves in the thatching. 'Ahu'ena heiau is now on the National Registry of Historic Places.

Commissioned by Henry Walker
Collection of Amfac/JMB Hawaii

KAMEHAMEHA SACRIFICING TO PELE

In 1801 a lava flow from Mt. Hualalai covered fishponds and villages for miles along the shoreline of North Kona.

When efforts by the priests to appease the volcano goddess Pele failed to stop the flow, Kamehameha traveled by canoe to Mahaiula, where the flow was entering the sea. At the edge of the flow he cut off some of his hair, wrapped it in a ti leaf and cast it into the lava, thus making a gift to Pele of a part of himself. This was the highest gift he could make; as a female spirit, Pele could not receive human sacrifice.

The flow stopped, and Mt. Hualalai has not erupted since.

Today subdivisions are spreading over the slopes of Hualalai despite warnings from scientists that the volcano is still active and an eruption is overdue. Kamehameha, however, is no longer available to propitiate Pele.

Collection of Robert Halsell

KA'AHUMANU

The favorite wife of Kamehameha, she was born in Hana, Maui, and raised in Kona, Hawai'i. Regarded by all as beautiful and spirited, Ka'ahumanu grew to six feet in height and at full maturity became prestigiously portly.

Her father, Ke'eaumoku, was the ruling chief of the Kona district, and a principal ally of Kamehameha. Indeed, it is doubtful that the rising young chief would have survived without his father-in-law's support.

Their marriage was not tranquil. She was impetuous and assertive; he, possessive and jealous. But in old age he found her to be the most trustworthy of anyone in his court. After his death in 1819, his son Liholiho became Kamehameha II, but Ka'ahumanu dominated the government as regent.

When Hawaiians crewing on foreign ships returned with tales of populous continents and powerful nations, it became clear that the kingdom must win recognition as a sovereign nation, or be devoured by some foreign power.

This motivated a desperate rush to become Europeanized as quickly as possible, which logically included accepting the European god. But abandoning the state religion brought civil war. Dissenting chiefs led by Kekuaokalani made a circuit of the island, assembling an army. Near Keauhou Bay, Kona they were defeated in a bloody battle. The old religion went out in a blaze of musket fire.

When missionaries arrived, she resisted them, refusing baptism until she had studied their ways for several years. Once a convert, however, she greatly aided their mission.

To consolidate semi-independent Kauai with the Monarchy of Hawai'i, she sailed there, invited King Kaumuali'i aboard, then sailed off, leaving the island without a ruler. She made him a prisoner with the tender chains of matrimony, but brutally suppressed a revolt on Kauai.

After Liholiho died of measles in London, Ka'ahumanu continued to rule until her death in 1832.

This painting is an attempt to reconstruct her appearance in the 1790s by removing the features of age seen in drawings done in her later years.

Artist's Collection

KAPI'OLANI DEFYING PELE

Left: In 1824 the high chiefess Kapi'olani, an ardent Christian, decided to act in defiance of Pele as a demonstration to her people of her new faith.

Ignoring dire warnings she descended into the caldera to the brink of the fire-pit Halema'uma'u. Here she ate 'ohelo berries without asking Pele's permission and read passages from the Bible.

Unharmed, she returned home, hopeful that her action would help win converts among her people.

Collection of Charles and Mavis Lavin

KAUIKEAOULI (KAMEHAMEHA III)

In his 1841 Constitution, he reaffirmed the tradition that the land was held by the chiefs and people in common, and that no man could own any part of it. Six years later, convinced by American advisors that land ownership would benefit his people, he undertook land distribution.

But Hawaiians did not comprehend land ownership, for how could mortals own something that was immortal? Much land quickly passed into foreign hands.

Collection of the Kamehameha Schools

PRINCESS BERNICE PAUAHI BISHOP

As one who did not sell her land, she bequeathed her entire estate to found and support a school for Hawaiian children—the Kamehameha Schools, known also as Bishop Estate. Her husband Charles Bishop left his personal estate to support the museum named in her memory.

Collection of The Kamehameha Schools

THE WHALER SUNBEAM OFF KA'ANAPALI, MAUI

Left: By the 1850s hundreds of whaling ships anchored each year in 'Lahaina Roads,' the sheltered waters off Lahaina and Ka'anapali—a popular place to get provisions, make repairs, recruit Hawaiian sailors, and give shore leave to weary crews.

Then, as now, humpback whales frequented these waters but were swift and difficult to catch. Whalers were more interested in larger species that produced more oil. There is, however, one record of Hawaiians bringing in a humpback.

Always eager to impress their colleagues, whaling ship captains would sail into Lahaina Roads under all plain sail, powered by the brisk trade-winds until they got into the lee of the island.

The ship in the painting is the *Sunbeam*, out of New Bedford. It sailed on its first voyage to the Indian Ocean and Pacific Ocean in 1856, and continued in service until 1909. A model of *Sunbeam* is displayed at the Whaling Museum at Whaler's Village, Ka'anapali.

Collection of the Maui Westin Hotel

THE STEAM SCHOONER *UPOLU*

Right: Owned by the Hind family of Kohala, the little *Upolu*, 93 feet long and 100 tons, carried goods and passengers between Upolu, Kohala, and Kealakekua Bay, Kona. Built in 1897 in Alameda, California, its two staterooms were occupied by members of the family on its eleven-day maiden voyage to Hawaii.

After four years of service, a new skipper, unfamiliar with the coastline and heedless of signals from Hawaiians on shore, ran it on the rocks at Puako.

Artist's Collection

CHURCH AT KAPA'AU, KOHALA, HAWAI'I ISLAND
Left: Collection of Robert and Puanani Van Dorpe

FATHER DAMIEN'S ARRIVAL AT KALAUPAPA
Right: In 1873 the Belgian priest answered his Bishop's call to work to ease the suffering of thousands dying of leprosy. Perhaps because he died of the disease in 1889, Damien is usually depicted as old and disfigured, but collector Pat Hopper suggested I portray him differently—as the vigorous, intense young priest who had been building churches on Hawai'i—resolute, yet appalled at what he saw at the moment he landed on Molokai.
Collection of Patrick W. Hopper

Herb Kawainui Kane
©1989

ON THE VERANDA
Collection of Nick G. Maggos

HUI-ALOHA CHURCH, KAUPO, MAUI
Right: Friends Carl and Rae Lindquist were among the many Maui folks whose dedication and volunteer work resulted in the restoration of this fine old church. It was also here that the owners of the painting were married. Is it only in imagination that one hears voices on the wind singing the old hymns?
Collection of Charles and Jane Wertz

Painting Portraits

In 1973 I was commissioned by C. Brewer, Ltd. to paint a portrait of the late Queen Salote of the Kingdom of Tonga. It was for presentation to the current Queen and Crown Princess, who were planning a visit to Hawai'i.

Portraits of those who have recently died are the devil to do because of the host of relatives and associates who knew them, each cherishing a different memory of the subject's physical appearance. While in Chicago I had painted, from photographs, a portrait of a recently-deceased corporation president for the company's boardroom, and had vowed never to do such a thing again. His surviving associates each did their helpful best to lead me in a different direction. I was not certain that I had made an end of it until it was presented to his widow, who, bursting into tears, cried "That's Charlie!" The comments of other critics were thus averted, but even the moment of success was nerve racking.

The same uncertainties were present in the assignment to portray Queen Salote. Photographs of the beloved and world-famous queen were so varied in their style and lighting that it was hard to believe that they were of the same person. Ultimately, I was guided as much by what I knew of her—by what I had heard of her gracious personality—as by the photographs.

I had just completed the work when the Queen's physician, along with some of her ladies-in-waiting, arrived in Honolulu to make preparations for her arrival. Upon learning that the physician had also served Salote for many years, I asked him to critique the portrait. He accompanied me to my studio, which at that time was in a little beach house in the Honolulu suburb of Kuliouou. He inspected the painting carefully, giving it his warm approval with some suggestions for slight changes in the eyes and hair. My deadline was at hand, and I needed a few days for the wet oil paints to set before the work could be moved. Promising to make the adjustments, I asked him to return the next day.

When he arrived, he studied the portrait without speaking.

"Do we have a likeness?" I asked.

He replied, "There are several ladies waiting outside who served Salote. Would you mind if they came in to see it?"

"I would be pleased."

He went to the door and spoke a few soft words in Tongan. Three smiling ladies quietly entered, each wearing the traditional fine mat around a very ample waist. The room suddenly seemed much smaller. When they hesitated just inside the doorway, I turned my easel so they might see the portrait.

HER ROYAL HIGHNESS SALOTE, QUEEN OF TONGA *(OPPOSITE)*
Collection of the Kingdom of Tonga

EDDIE KAMAE
Above: Virtuoso of the ukulele and leader of the "Sons of Hawai'i," Eddie Kamae is also a musicologist whose tireless interviewing and collecting has saved many old songs which would otherwise have been lost.
Artist's Collection

AUNTY CLARA
She lived at Honaunau Bay in South Kona. When we anchored *Hokule'a* there on its first training and shakedown cruise, she insisted on sailing with us when we left. I could not refuse her.

She became the beloved elder of our crew, who made a seat for her before the mizzen mast. While in port on Maui and Molokai she lived aboard as self-appointed guardian of the vessel, keeping a sharp eye on mischievous children. After we arrived in Honolulu, she kissed me goodbye and said "Mahalo, Captain. Now I can die happy."

None of us knew about her illness until cancer claimed her a few months later. Her last words were "Hokule'a! Hokule'a!"
Collection of Stephen Lenci

CYRUS GREEN *Collection of Mary Green*

I saw a flash of recognition in their eyes. Then, without a word, they assumed the traditional posture of respect when approaching Polynesian royalty. On hands and knees, they crawled into the room.

The physician smiled, "Does that answer your question?"

"It does," I said, "and thank you *very* much."

A portrait is not like any other sort of painting. It is a picture in which the subject matter is a unique resemblance, an image created by looking at the subject from a special point of view. To get this likeness, which must be more than a simple representation of the sitter, a peculiar state of empathy toward the subject must be established and maintained throughout the painter's performance. Not even the more experienced portraitists really understand how this is done. With some sitters it comes easily; with others, never. If it exists, the portrait will look like the sitter whether it is well or poorly painted. If it cannot be developed, the painting can never advance beyond a caricature.

Portraits are traditionally done at a distance of from four to eight feet from the subject. A likeness may be obtained from closer or farther away, but it will not have that peculiar quality of a portrait, a sort of communication that a viewer may hold with the figure in the painting. Most portraits which appear to be life size are actually 3/4 life size. That's the size a person appears while at a comfortable distance of six feet from the painter, close enough so that the sitter can be seen clearly, yet not so close that the artist's vision becomes distorted. That this is also the distance of good conversation may have something to do with establishing that communication between portrait and viewer.

Full length portraits were traditionally done by placing the canvas on an easel set next to the sitter, with the painter standing about fourteen feet away to view both canvas and sitter together, walking forward to place each series of brush strokes, then returning to the vantage point, until the full figure was blocked in. The face would be painted later with the canvas at arms reach, the easel set about eight feet from the sitter. This approach avoided the false perspective, the appearance of a tilted floor which working too closely can give—a distortion seen in photos made with wide-angle lenses.

Like most artists today, I work from photos, but if the portrait is of a living person, I prefer to do the photography myself. Then each picture is a reminder of a view personally experienced, something quite different from a photograph taken by someone else. Photography has made it possible to do portraits that could not otherwise be done. On more than one occasion a jealous husband has been comforted by the knowledge that I was working on a portrait of his wife largely from photographs, at a safe distance from the sitter. Only once did a husband insist that I do a portrait of his wife entirely from life; then, although both were twice my age, he sat in a corner of my studio, his cane grasped firmly in hand, and glared at me throughout every sitting.

Children are difficult to photograph, being too much aware of the camera. One must point the camera at them and click the shutter repeat-

IOLANI LUAHINE (1915-1978)
Hawai'i's foremost exponent of the dance.

When she danced, she was the spirit of the dance. When she chanted, she was the poet of the Hawaiian soul.

Whenever she stopped by my Kona studio, it meant that I was finished working for the day—it was party time.

Hawai'i is infinitely richer for her having lived among us.

Collection of Charles "Imua" Forward

GABBY PAHINUI *Collection of the Pahinui Family*

edly until they become bored with it and turn their attention elsewhere. That is when I load the film.

Women of middle age are the most difficult portrait clients if they have not yet become resigned to their years. In her mirror, each still sees the girl in her twenties that she once was. No honest likeness will please them, and they can easily find others who will agree that the artist has missed the mark.

Most men will not object to features of age that may add character to their faces. They are usually less interested in handsome appearance, but more interested in portraiture which conveys some impression of their status. Everyone who has passed forty seems to think of himself or herself as a mature young person. Nobody can know how he or she is seen by others. This is why the portrait painter is often frightening to his sitter; and why each may find the other so difficult and sometimes so impossible to forgive.

There have always been a few very facile "society" portrait painters who know this very well, who are able to mirror the subject's self esteem in the standard of glamor that happens to be fashionable at the time. Their portraits may resemble Hollywood clones, and may look quaint or even ludicrous as soon as fashions change, but they can at least console themselves with their fees.

I think it was Sir Joshua Reynolds who said that when faced with a difficult female subject, he always painted the most beautiful face he could imagine; then added only those adjustments necessary to make it resemble the sitter.

JUDSON BROWN
An elder leader and historian of the Tlingit Nation of Alaska, Brown was a fisherman who became a leader in the long struggle for civil rights and reparations. His wisdom continues to inspire cultural revival among the people of Northwest Coast Indian nations.
Artist's Collection

BEAR DANCER
A dancer at a cultural celebration in Juneau, Alaska.
Artist's Collection

PUANANI MAKING KAPA

The making of bark cloth from the white inner bark of the paper mulberry and other trees was widespread in Polynesia. Originally known as *tapa*, it is pronounced *kapa* in Hawai'i, where the art reached its highest refinement, often made up of several paper-thin layers sewn together with the facing layer beautifully decorated.

Kapa was primarily used for garments, sleeping coverings, and for wrapping precious objects, with the finest being offered as gifts symbolic of rank and prestige.

Successive beatings of the bark combined with complicated soaking and fermenting processes to soften it produced wide strips. The strips were then enlarged by overlapping their edges and beating them into large seamless sheets.

Designs known as watermarks were often impressed into the material in a final beating with beaters incised with intricate designs. *Kapa* was dyed and pigmented in many colors, and elaborate designs of great variety were added by stamping, stenciling, or brushing.

With the importation of European cloth, the unique art of Hawaiian *kapa* withered, and the processes were forgotten. Now the art is being revived as a cherished legacy.

The leading experimenter and practitioner is Puanani Van Dorpe, depicted in this painting at work in her studio. For over fourteen years she has patiently gathered old accounts of *kapa* processes and put them to actual test, carefully recording and evaluating the results of each experiment. Through arduous practice she has also developed the skills for beating, watermarking, and decorating, and she is now able to produce *kapa* that is identical to *kapa* produced centuries ago. She has shared her discoveries with others, and a growing interest on the part of art collectors may further stimulate the revival of this almost-lost art.

She has taught others. In 1989 she enlisted the help of other Hawaiian women to make 1,000 pieces of *kapa* for the respectful reburial of human remains excavated by archaeologists from an ancient site.

Collection of Virginia Mathis

RICHARD LYMAN

Left: President of the Kamehameha Schools and an elder statesman for the Hawaiian people, the late Richard Lyman was also a strong advocate of reforestation, as illustrated here by his pruning a young koa tree.

Collection of Mrs. Richard Lyman

PELE, GODDESS OF HAWAI'I'S VOLCANOES

Right: One of the most dramatic gods of the Hawaiian mythology, Pele lives in Hawaiian hearts and minds as the supreme personification of volcanic majesty and power. Within the Hawaiian cosmos all natural forces are regarded as life forces, related to humanity by common descent from the same ultimate creative spirits.

Possessing the power to create new land, Pele also has a volcanic personality. She is by nature impetuous and lusty, jealous, unpredictable,and capable of sudden fury and great violence. She can also be gentle, loving, and as serene as her forests of ferns and flowering trees.

Born in the awe experienced by an ancient people, she still makes her presence felt by those who visit her domain today.

Collection of William and Kahala Ann Trask Gibson

PELE *Collection of Barry Moore*

A Portrait of Pele

THIS PAINTING BEGAN with many unsuccessful attempts to express my interpretation of Pele's personality. The idea had been bothering me for some time, and over a period of several months, I made many sketches in pencil. All were failures. None said, "I am Pele."

One morning I arrived in my studio and again started a sketch—and another—and another. The day's scheduled work was forgotten. I disconnected the phone. A scattering of unsatisfactory sketches began to litter the floor.

Then I began perspiring. It was one of those all too rare moments when the pencil or brush seems to move itself. The face I had been looking for suddenly appeared.

I whispered, "There you are!"

I quickly traced it down on a canvas that had been intended for another painting, washed an underpainting over the surface, and began to develop that face.

She hung around my studio for just a few weeks before a friend tore her away from me. He had dropped by to tell me about a new girl friend, and here he found another.

Months later Ranger Jon Erickson called from Hawai'i Volcanoes National Park, asking me to participate with their designers on a new museum about Hawai'i's volcanoes. It had been conceived as a scientific museum, but something seemed missing; science alone could not express the *human experience* of the volcanoes.

Pele personified that experience. I worked with the designers to integrate paintings of the Hawaiian volcano myths with the scientific presentations. The design phase was successful.

For the museum depictions of Pele I searched for a model. At breakfast one morning at the Hotel Hana Maui I thought I saw the features I was looking for in the face of our waitress. When I introduced myself to her, she replied...

"Yes, I know who you are. I'm Mona Ling, the daughter of Sam Kalalau who sailed with you on *Hokule'a*."

She modelled for me in a photo session that afternoon. Later I developed some of the poses into several studies, and further developed one of the studies into the painting *On the Lanai* in this book. But when I did the paintings of Pele for the new Jaggar Museum, I found that none of the photos of Mona worked for me. Although she had the same strong, beautiful Hawaiian face, I discovered that I could not convert her features into a portrait that would say "I am Pele." So all my paintings and sculpture of Pele have been done, like the first, not from a human model, but from the vision in my mind's eye. I can only believe that it was because Mona's features were just too vulnerably *human*.

After the museum paintings were done and I was putting away my research, it occurred to me that here was material that might be molded into a little book. *Pele, Goddess of Hawai'i's Volcanoes,* was published a year later in 1987.

PELE DREAMING
Bronze bas-relief 34" in diameter. Limited edition

PELE'S VOYAGE TO HAWAI'I

From Tahiti comes the woman, Pele
From the land of Bora Bora
From the rising mist of Kane, dawn swelling,
From the clouds blazing over Tahiti

Left: Guided by her elder brother Kamohoali'i in the form of a great shark, Pele voyaged with brothers and sisters in a great canoe from the ancient homeland. Some say she yearned to travel. Others whisper that she was driven out by a great flood caused by her elder sister, a sea goddess, outraged because Pele had seduced her husband.

She carried her little sister Hi'iaka in the shape of an egg. Pele's favorite, the gentle and beautiful Hi'iaka emerged from her egg shape in Hawai'i and became a spirit of the dance. Many traditional hula performances are dedicated to Hi'iaka and to Pele.

Collection of William and Kahala Ann Trask Gibson

A PANTHEON OF VOLCANO SPIRITS

At right:

From left to right: Kamapua'a, the hog god; a mischievous spirit of rain and plant life. Pele's lover, but in all ways her opposite. Theirs was a stormy relationship.

Poliahu, goddess of snowy Mauna Kea and a rival to Pele.

Pele's sisters, Kapo and Laka, two personalities of the same spirit— one a spirit of fertility and sorcery, the other a spirit of the dance.

Hi'iaka, a spirit of the dance, was Pele's favorite.

Pele.

Ka-moho-ali'i, respected elder brother and keeper of the water of life. As a great shark he led Pele to Hawaii.

Lonomakua, keeper of the sacred fire sticks, made volcanic fires at Pele's command.

Ka-poho-i-kahi-ola, spirit of explosions.

Ke-ua-a-ke-po, spirit of the rain of fire.

Kane-hekili, spirit of thunder.

Ke-o-ahi-kama-kaua, spirit of lava fountains.

Collection of William and Kahala Ann Trask Gibson

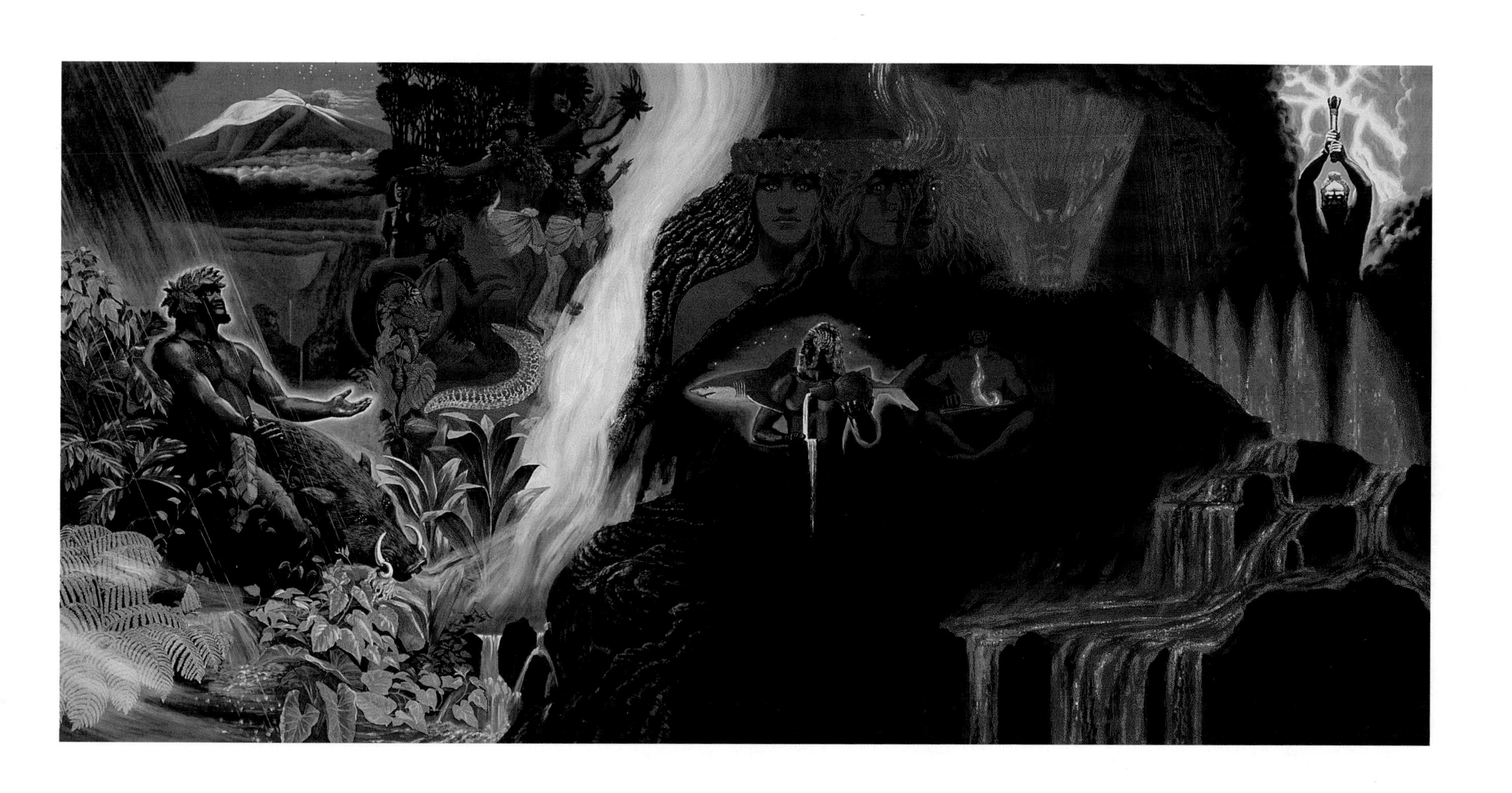

ESCAPE FROM PELE
When a proud chief was challenged to a *holua* race by a strange woman, his refusal was less than polite. Literally inflamed by her wrath, she pursued him riding a flow of lava. Only his skill saved him. At the seashore he sailed for Maui, never to return.
Artist's Collection

HOLUA!

HOLUA, a sport of chiefs, involved launching a sled with long wooden runners down a runway constructed of rockwork. A layer of small pebbles was placed over the rockwork, and for the actual sledding a layer of slippery thatching was added. The sport seems to have died out in the early 19th century, possibly losing its reason for existence when the annual makahiki festival was abandoned in 1819.

Though the sport has obvious dangers, no account has survived to pass on details of the composition of the thatching or the speed of the sleds. Conventional wisdom holds that the sleds moved on a slippery surface of layers of grass or broad leaves of ti and banana, but within living memory no one had actually tested this. While planning a painting of holua sledding, in which the thatching was to be depicted, I decided to make the test myself.

What remains of the great *holua* slide of Kaneaka (kah-ney-ah-KAH) still stands in Keauhou, in the Kona district of Hawai'i. Once a straight, mile-long stone ramp descending to the sea, the lower half has been demolished to make room for condos and a golf course.

One ancient sled survives in the Bishop Museum. Knowing what the curator's response would be if I proposed to borrow it, I mocked-up a sled out of a few boards, and, with a large trash bag filled with grass and banana leaves, climbed up the remaining 3,000 feet of the slide.

It is an amazing piece of work, a massive rock structure 50 feet wide, in some places raised as much as 11 feet above the old lava flow beneath it. Most of the original surface paving of small lava pebbles has now disappeared, trampled by cattle and shaken down among the larger rocks by earthquakes; but near the top I found an area where the pebble paving still existed. I shingled a length of this with grass and leaves, got above it, and threw myself down on the sled.

Disaster! My weight pressed the sled runners down through the grass, where they were gripped by the rough lava pebbles and brought to a grinding stop. I continued onward, off the sled and on into the "rough."

There was a cackle of hilarity from mynah birds in the bushes nearby, but I was not amused. Obviously something was missing in the folklore. Some kind of cushioning must have been laid between the grass and the gravel. A layer of earth, well beaten down, may have been used elsewhere, but not in rocky Kona where soil was precious. One hard rain would wash it down into the rockwork of the slide.

Then I thought of the mats. In the old days, when men did the cooking and all heavy work, about all women had to do was care for children, and engage in such womanly crafts as making *kapa* (bark cloth), and plaiting *lauhala* mats from strips of long pandanus leaves. Working in congenial, gossipy groups, they turned out thousands of mats—fine mats to sleep upon, coarse floor mats, strips of matting for canoe sails, heavy mats that commoners carried in battle as armor against stones and spears—mats for a multitude of purposes. The rockwork platforms of thatched Hawaiian houses were covered with many layers of mats. When a floor mat became frayed beyond respectability, a new one was laid over it. In any Hawaiian village there were huge quantities of old floor mats, which, to satisfy a chiefly whim, could be quickly brought out and laid up on a *holua* slide.

Stored under my house were some old mats gathering mould and termites. I hauled these up the slide along with several trash bags of grass cut from a rancher's pasture. Cutting the mats into wide strips, I shingled these over the pebbled surface of the slide, and laid the grass over them. Then, holding the sled before me, I made a short sprint and once again threw myself into the experiment.

Terminal velocity! But in that same instant I saw that I really hadn't prepared for the experiment being such a success. It was a thrilling ride so long as the mats held out, but then I shot over the last strip of matting. The bare rocks gripped the sled, I was briefly airborn, then on the rocks myself—lava rocks with lots of sharp edges.

Later, while applying peroxide and band-aids, I was consoled by the thought that data derived from experiment was, in the absence of historical knowledge, acceptable. But with all due respect for the scientific method, this was one experiment that I was not about to confirm by repetition.

A Treasure Ship of the Ming Navy

WITH ORDERS to "show kindness to people of distant places," early Ming Dynasty Admiral Zheng He commanded seven voyages (1405 - 1433 A.D.) throughout the Indian Ocean, and Indonesia, carrying gifts to more than thirty governments. Foreign ambassadors bearing gifts were brought to China. Trade was stimulated.

This was voyaging on a colossal scale involving battleships, troop ships, cavalry ships, supply ships, and treasure ships. The treasure ships were the largest wooden ships in history—a recorded length of 440 feet seems confirmed by the recent unearthing of a rudder post 35 feet long at the shipyard site at Nanjing. The fourth voyage, 1413-1415, included 63 large vessels, many smaller ships, and almost 28,000 men.

Such massive forces quickly crushed anyone opposing them. A king of pirates was defeated in a sea battle, clearing the trade route to the Indian Ocean. The king of Ceylon was captured in a land battle and taken to China for pardon by the emperor. The fleet visited India, Arabia, Persia, and East Africa—where Ming porcelain remains a decorative element in the masonry of many old buildings. A contemporary map suggests that the Chinese may have sailed around Africa's southern cape and into the Atlantic. Had the momentum of Chinese exploration continued, they would have reached Europe before Columbus sailed westward on his search for a new route to China.

After the death of the Emperor, his successor was persuaded by an anti-maritime faction to abandon exploration and forbid trading expeditions by Chinese vessels—a decision which altered the course of world history. Later, when Europeans began exploring the Indian Ocean, they heard tales of immense ships, so huge they seemed incredible.

Chinese shipwrights built hulls of successive layers of sheathing reinforced with interior bulkheads, a method which equals the strength of steel and permits vessels of great size. Chinese inventions include the stern rudder, watertight compartments, leeboards, fully battened sails, gunpowder, cannon, and the magnetic compass.

Contemporary depictions of these ships were probably destroyed, along with many other records of this era, by the anti-maritime faction. This painting may be the most careful pictorial reconstruction done to date. It is based on surviving descriptions of the treasure ships, a general study of ships from the Sung through the Ming Dynasties, and a conjectural model built at the Institute of Navigation of Jimei now in a Nanjing museum. The most informative English language source on the treasure ships is Joseph Needham's *Science and Civilization in China*. My own research of this subject was supported by the National Geographic Society.

MEMBERS OF THE WEDDING
(a.k.a. The Family Board of Directors)
Left: Most often in Hawaiian families the '*tutu*-ladies', grandmothers and elderly aunties, have the last word. Always given the best seats at family gatherings, they form a stationary center around which the activities of their children and grandchildren orbit. Hawaiians revere their *kupuna* (elders) as custodians of the old ways, sources of wisdom, and living links to their ancestors.
Collection of Nick G. Maggos

LEI SELLERS *(Below left)*
Collection of the Chart House, Inc.

NOTES

1. *(Page 16)* Mentors have always been long on advice, if short on example. In his *The Book on Art*, the 14th century painter Cennino Cennini advised young artists to avoid rich foods and heavy wines, and to spare the hand "*...from such strains as heaving stones, crowbars, and many other things which are bad for your hand, from giving them a chance to weary it. There is another cause which, if you indulge it, can make your hand so unsteady that it will waver more, and flutter far more, than leaves do in the wind, and this is indulging too much in the company of women.*"

2. *(Page 20)* The three volumes of *Canoes of Oceania* were combined and reprinted in 1975 as Bishop Museum Special Publication 27. James Hornell was a British fisheries expert whose work in the Pacific during the early 20th century put him in contact with what remained of the canoe culture. Collaborating with him on this monumental work was A. C. Haddon, an Oxford scholar who conducted a world-wide survey of archival materials.

3. *(Page 30)* Was Polynesian exploration and settlement intentional, involving planned voyages? Or, accidental as the result of storm-wrecked canoes drifting off course or on one-way voyages of exile? The two views overlap insofar as all

THE OLD MAN AND THE SEA
Hawaiian fishermen in small canoes often searched far offshore for the pelagic fish of the open sea. The skillful were held in high esteem. Hundreds of Hawaiian terms for fish species, ocean currents, weather phenomena, and sea conditions attest to the scope of their knowledge and their intimacy with nature.
Collection of Dallas Jensen

discoveries are fortuitous, but they differ radically in their estimates of the accuracy of Polynesian navigation and their assessment of the seaworthiness and windward performance of Polynesian canoes.

The argument heated up in the 1950s and 1960s. The "intentional voyages" proponents were accused of being too romantic about Polynesian maritime capabilities, too quick to accept the voyaging legends; and the "accidental drift" theorists were accused of being overly eurocentric, unable to accept the idea that anyone except Europeans could accomplish great feats of exploration, and those only in vessels that fell within the modern definition of 'seaworthy.'

The "accidental drift" theory was shot down by computer simulations of wind patterns and ocean currents which concluded that a drifting canoe had no chance of reaching Hawai'i, Easter Island, and New Zealand from other parts of Polynesia or Micronesia.

The route between Tahiti and Hawaii passes through three ocean currents and requires sailing slightly against the wind both ways. Could the ancient voyaging canoes perform well enough to windward to make round trips? *Hokule'a's* 1976 round trip voyage proved that they could. And the navigation experiments conducted in 1976 and in subsequent voyages have proved the adequacy of Polynesian navigation.

4. (p. 32) The time came to name the canoe. Anthropologist Kenneth Emory reminded us that this was traditionally done by the chief designer who received the name in a dream.

On a clear night early in 1975 I spent several hours studying the stars. After retiring, I dreamed of stars. Arcturus suddenly grew brighter, until its intensity forced me awake. Before I went back to sleep I scribbled *'Hokule'a'* (Hawaiian for Arcturus) on the notepad on my nightstand. Noticing the note in the morning, it struck me that this would be an appropriate name for the canoe. The name was proposed and received unanimous approval.

Suppose you are sailing north from Tahiti, seeking Hawai'i without radio or navigation instruments. You will notice that as Arcturus arches from east to west in the night sky the top of its arch, its zenith, becomes higher as you sail northward. You prudently sail somewhat to windward to compensate for the leeward drift of your vessel, and to gain sufficient 'easting' to arrive at Hawai'i's latitude upwind of your destination. When Arcturus passes directly overhead, you are on the same latitude as Hawai'i. You can then turn downwind, keeping the rising sun aft, the setting sun forward, the zenith of Arcturus directly overhead, and you will make landfall at Hawai'i.

Which is probably why some ancient navigator named that star *Hokule'a*—star of gladness.

5. (p.37) Ask why peoples of diverse racial and ethnic backgrounds are capable of living and working in relative harmony in Hawai'i, while peoples in other parts of the world are killing each other over relatively minor differences, and most folks here will simply say "It's the aloha spirit."

The term has been diluted by the visitor industry. But within the context of Hawai'i's history it might be defined as an open friendliness and hospitality, a selfless concern for others, that may be universal within clans or extended families everywhere, but which in Hawaii has been extended to all persons of good will, regardless of their race or culture.

Once they were exposed to the outside world, Hawaiians learned that people who live upon small, isolated islands, must be open to borrowing ideas, things, and even genes from outside their shores, else they will become static, and decline. Most of the early foreign residents in Hawaii were adventurous young men from Europe, America, and China, and of those who stayed, and proved to be men of good will, many were accepted by marriage into Hawaiian families.

Intermarriage became a survival mechanism for the Hawaiian people. Although little was then known about immunities, it was observed that part Hawaiian children were more likely to survive epidemics than children of pure Hawaiian parents.

Hawaiian was the language of government for most of the 19th century. Immigrants from different parts of the world learned Hawaiian in order to communicate with each other. The Hawaiian culture, as the host culture, had a softening effect on those who came here, knocking off rough edges that could have become destructively abrasive. And when peoples of vastly different backgrounds began sharing grandchildren, their differences began to seem less important.

Perhaps only when peoples can enjoy their differences as a resource of cultural enrichment do they become truly civilized.

6. *(Page 38)* Current (1990-91) auction results are embarrassing proof that the market for publicity-inflated contemporary art—now in free-fall after the boom of the 1980s—is more volatile than the market for art that has been tested by time.

7. *(Page 47)* Some of the differences between primal and modern thought are discussed in "Worlds Apart" (p. 158)

8. *(Page 59)* Archaeology in Kahana Valley, Oahu, has produced pollen of kukui, ti, and taro—Polynesian plants which had to have been brought by canoe. Other evidence includes charcoal from apparently man-made burn-offs and marine shells. The shells indicate a change in the lower valley from a marine environment to a valley floor built by alluvial deposits resulting from agricultural activity. The evidence, indicating settlement by the first century A.D. and possibly earlier, is discussed in Patricia Price Beggerly, Ph.D. Dissertation, Anthropology Dept., University of Hawai'i, 1990: *Kahana Valley, Hawai'i; a Geomorphic Artifact: A Study of the Interrelationships among Geomorphic Structures, Natural Processes, and Ancient Hawaiian Technology, Land Use, and Settlement Pattern.*

9. *(Page 61)* The most comprehensive survey of Polynesian traditions of exploration and settlement is *Vikings of the Pacific,* Peter H. Buck, (University of Chicago Press 1959, Fourth Impression 1967).

10. *(Page 74)* For more about Anson's voyage: *Anson's Voyage*, L.A. Wilcox, (G. Bell & Sons, London, 1969); *Documents Relating to Anson's Voyage Round the World,* Glyndwr Williams, The Navy Records Society, London, 1967.

11. *(Page 76) Journal of William Ellis* (Advertiser Publishing Co., Ltd., 1963) pp. 319-320).

12. *(Page 76)* Polynesians were usually hostile at first contact with Europeans arriving in what appeared to be threatening numbers, sometimes prefacing the hostility with deceptive acts of friendship. But a few helpless survivors of shipwreck, posing no threat, might be received with kindness—after they had been stripped of any belongings.

13. *(Page 76)* For more on the Manila Galleons: "Track of the Manila Galleons", Eugene Lyons, *National Geographic* (September 1990). Lyons, Director of the Center for Historic Research, the St. Augustine Foundation, Flagler College, St. Augustine, is perhaps the foremost researcher on this corner of history, and in further research will continue to keep an eye on the question of Spanish sighting of the Hawaiian archipelago (personal communication).

14. *(Page 79)* For the writings of Cook and excerpts from the journals of his officers during their time in the Hawaiian Islands, see: *The Journals of Captain Cook,* Vol. III, Parts One and Two, J.C. Beaglehole, Ed., (Hakluyt Society 1967). An excellent, well-illustrated narrative of the events is found in *Captain Cook in Hawai'i,* Terence Barrow, (Island Heritage, Ltd., 1976).

15. *(Page 84)* A description and ethnologist's interpretation of the makahiki is found in *Islands of History*, Marshall Sahlins (University of Chicago Press 1985).

16. *(Page 88)* Cook's illness may not have been entirely caused by the fatigue of command. A British physician suggests that his erratic and sometimes irrational behavior during the last months of his life—including the rash act which led to his death—may be attributed to vitamin B deprivation caused by intestinal parasites. "Medical Aspects and Consequences of Cook's Voyages", Sir James Watt, in *Captain James Cook and his Times*, Robin Fisher & Hugh Johnston, editors, (University of Washington Press, 1979)—papers from a bicentennial symposium on Cook's explorations held at Simon Fraser University, British Columbia, in 1978.

17. *(Page 90)* For a fascinating account of how the Cook legend was mythicised in Britain—his elevation to the status of a Promethean hero bestowing the blessings of European civilization upon the primitive peoples of Oceania— see also "Cook's Posthumous Reputation," Bernard Smith, in *Captain Cook and his Times* (cited above).

18. *(Page 91)* For a full description of the efforts by American missionaries to discredit Cook, see: "Origin of the Condemnation of Captain Cook in Hawaii," by John F.G. Stokes, *39th Annual Report of the Hawaiian Historical Society*, 1930.

19. *(Page 98) Before the Horror, The Population of Hawaii on the Eve of Western Contact*, David E. Stannard, (Social Science Research Institute, 1989, distributed by the University of Hawaii Press).

In this first multi-disciplined study of the subject, Stannard draws on archaeology, demography, comparative history, ethnology, geography, botany, and physiology to suggest a 1778 population of at least 800,000, reduced to a scant 40,000 a century later.

When first confronted with this information the usual response is "How could such a staggering population collapse occur with so little recorded mention of it?"

One reason is that little recording was done during the first half century after contact. Missionary records of the continued decline after the 1820s have been largely ignored. We can only assume that there was an amnesia about it. For both Hawaiians and non-Hawaiians, each for their own reasons, it was a subject too terrible to think about.

20. *(Page 104)* The most authoritative sources on the activities of the ruling chiefs and life in their courts are the writings of three Hawaiian historians: David Malo, John Papa I'i, and Samuel M. Kamakau. Malo and I'i were raised in the court of Kamehameha I.

21. *(Page 112)* The Journal of James Morrison has been published in French, but not in English except in a limited edition of only 500 copies (Golden Cockerel Press, 1935).

22. *(Page 115)* The book referred to by National Geographic's researcher is *The Armed Transport Bounty*, John McKay, (Conway Maritime Press, London, and Naval Institute Press, Annapolis, 1989). It is a book in the popular series *The Anatomy of the Ship*.

23. *(Page 124)* Perhaps the most complete biography of Vancouver is *Vancouver, A Life, 1757-1798*, George Godwin, (Philip Allan, London, 1930).

Vancouver's journal, *A Voyage of Discovery to the North Pacific Ocean and Round the World*, have been re-published by the Hakluyt Society, London.

A Reference Work on Pacific Maritime History

For readers interested in the history of sailing ships in the Pacific, I warmly recommend *Pacific Sail, Four Centuries of Western Ships in the Pacific*, Roger Morris (David Bateman, Ltd., Auckland, 1987). Roger Morris is a maritime artist-historian and a professional seaman of broad experience in sailing ships. The book is loaded with superb paintings and fascinating information, all carefully researched and accurate.

LADIES OF THE AHAHUI KA'AHUMANU

Honoring the name of a dynamic queen, the Ka'ahumanu Society keeps the language and womanly crafts of old Hawai'i. With royal dignity they hold fast to the graceful attributes of our culture, guarding them from the relentless impact of waves of change that beat upon our island shores.

Collection of Robert Halsell

WORLDS APART

When the 18th Century British expedition under Capt. Cook arrived in Hawai'i, differences of world view and logic between the two cultures often made mutual understanding impossible. Actions that were perfectly rational to one group often seemed bizarre or incomprehensible to the other. Hawai'i was not unique. Throughout the world, wherever the emerging modern European culture collided with a culture rooted in a primal past, the same gulf of incomprehension existed.

The Awakening of the Individual

But only a few centuries earlier Cook's Viking ancestors, conquerors of England, were of a primal society essentially similar to that of the Polynesian Hawaiians—a similarity revealed by their mythologies. The myths of any people form a self portrait of those who invented them, and the fundamental universality of these stories reveals a startling sameness among primal societies.

How had European culture become so incompatible with earlier cultures? To discover what had stimulated a market economy, innovation, rapid acculturation in science and technology, new political experiments—all that would become the 'modern' culture as we know it—we must look back to what has been called 'The Dawn of Humanism', which we may take to mean the emergence of individual self-awareness, followed by the assertion of individual rights.

In primal societies kinship loyalties override self-awareness. Individuals regard themselves primarily as functional components of an extended family or clan. 'We' overrides 'me.' The clan's status and survival are the individual's primary concerns. Production and trade are controlled by clan leaders; monopolized by ruling families as societies become larger and more stratified.

In medieval Europe trade was the monopoly of kings or emperors, as it has always been throughout the kingdoms and empires of the East. But Europe's rulers were often illiterate, chronically insecure, preoccupied with chivalry, galloping off on crusades, or in other ways too ineffective to control commerce. Only among Europe's petty states could an individual of humble station begin to dream of holding unto himself the wealth that he might accumulate, investing it, and becoming a self-directing, self-serving capitalist.

Perhaps the Jews of Europe, forbidden to own land or engage in many of the crafts, their survival limited to whatever might be done with portable property, may have showed the way to others.

It was a radical idea, and we know that European rulers took a dim view of it. Individual rights to own property and conduct trade were dearly bought during the Middle Ages, often literally purchased as franchises by emerging merchant societies, paid for in gold to cash-hungry kings or princes, and not infrequently with blood when rulers changed their minds.

But once the thing was done, an assertive middle class developed, among them new "merchant princes."

We look back on humanism as a flowering of philosophy, the arts and sciences, founded upon a new and secular awakening of man to his own humanity. More to the point, it was the individual's awakening to self awareness, and the political creation of rights by which an individual could attend to his self interest.

Innovation, discouraged in primal societies, now fueled a burgeoning market economy. The new merchant class learned that investment in science, technology, and exploration could produce new inventions, new markets, and greater profits. A scientific and industrial revolution was born. And after Galileo and Newton, the European world view would be forever changed, with no turning back. When Captain Cook reached Hawaii, the primal mythology of Europe was being replaced with a mythology of the future; but not without discomforts and contradictions that persist today.

In the same decade of Cook's death, those individual rights which had been unthinkable a few centuries earlier, then wrung from rulers with great sacrifice, had become so ingrained that they were proclaimed by the activists of the American Revolution as 'self evident' and 'inalienable.'

And today? In the modern 'free world' these are now 'civil' or 'constitutional' rights at home, 'human' rights abroad. We trumpet them to others, but while peoples of totalitarian or third world nations are certainly attentive to the products of modern culture, the rights and responsibilities inherent to self-directed individualism may be only dimly comprehended. Perhaps the major obstacle to America's world-wide human rights mission is the same empathy gap that existed between the 18th century British and Hawaiians—the inability of each party to see through the eyes of the other.

Some Differences between 'Primal' and Modern Societies

The Polynesian example, used here for illustration, was essentially similar to other primal societies despite Hawai'i's position as the most isolated in the world.

The Universe

Perceived as fixed, perfect, eternal, with change limited to seasonal and life cycles, their universe was an organic whole of which each thing or person was an integral part. Success depended upon living in harmony with Nature's equilibrium.

Disciplined to preserving the status quo, primal societies have an abhorrence of fundamental change that may result in refusal to adapt to modern thinking even after their cultures have disintegrated. Such rigidity makes their cultures brittle, easily shattered when impacted by the more resilient and dynamic modern culture.

In the modern view the universe is impermanent and ever changing, with man having no integral position within it. This view weakens pressures for conformity, and produces a fluid social climate adaptive to change, often thriving on it—a climate in which individuals have less emotional security, less sense of belonging or of place, but a far greater array of freedoms and choices.

Natural and Supernatural

Polynesians apparently had no concept of the supernatural as a sphere separate from Nature. Gods and spirits were their natural ancestors, as well as the progenitors of everything in the universe; hence humankind was related by ancestry to everything else.

Religion was so integrated with life that no separate word for it was needed. Revering the original creators as their ultimate ancestors, Polynesians would have found the modern idea of a conquest of Nature to be incomprehensible, patricidal, and certain to bring terrible retribution from natural forces. Within this ecological world-view, Polynesians strove to know Nature intimately and live harmoniously within it.

The modern religious view sees the supernatural and natural as two distinct spheres, with man somewhere in between, but *above* Nature. A conquest of Nature is regarded as man's manifest destiny, if not his God-given right.

Seniority

In primal cultures all authority is based on seniority. Older brothers rule younger; clan elders rule the extended family; chiefly families rule commoner families by genealogical seniority, claiming more direct descent from the original gods. The highest gods are senior to lesser spirits.

The modern world may tolerate distinctions based on seniority, but it can thrive only where individuals may advance upon their own merits.

The static nature of primal societies benefited the status of elders whose accumulated knowledge was still relevant in old age. But in the modern world rapid changes result in generation gaps and human obsolescence; elders lose usefulness, status, and self-esteem.

Conformity vs Individuality

In a Norse legend of Viking ships racing to attack England, a chief, eager that the ship of his clan have the honor of touching English soil first, drew his sword, cut off his hand, and threw it to shore ahead of the other ships. This act is incomprehensible to modern individualists, but it illustrates the primal value of selflessness.

As in other primal societies, Polynesians placed the clan's collective interest over self interest. Individuality was discouraged if not punished.

Modern culture, however, is led by individual initiative, flourishing where governments define and protect individual rights. Yet in many societies, including contemporary Polynesian society, a residue of the primal conformity impulse persists which often discourages individual advancement.

Should surplus earnings be invested for individual gain at the risk of being considered stingy, or should they be distributed to benefit others in the clan, thus sacrificing personal wealth for psychic income? This dilemma is a major obstacle to Polynesian entrepreneurship.

In Fiji, I learned that any gift to a housemaid is turned over to her husband or a clan elder upon her return home, unless it is accompanied by a note insisting that it be for her alone. The gift might then be offered to the village chief, who might keep it or return it with his compliments. It's more rewarding to gain honor by offering the gift than to keep it.

The primal roots of modern Russian society are evident in the active resentment displayed by many against those few who have begun to achieve wealth by asserting their new rights as individuals.

Land

As in many other primal cultures there was no concept of land ownership in Polynesia. If the land was immortal, how could mortals own land? Land could not belong to men because men belonged to the land.

In most Pacific Islands today, Hawaii and Guam excepted, land either cannot be sold, or can be bought by outsiders only with severe restrictions. In many Pacific nations the lands are largely controlled by chiefs operating as native land trusts.

SISTERS
Girls at a country luau at Punalu'u Beach in the Ka'u district of Hawai'i Island, 1973
Collection of Matson Navigation

The Power of Words

Modern culture and democracy could not exist without broad dissemination of information. The written word is the vehicle of power. But writing was not invented in Polynesia because the very idea of its result, the uncontrolled dissemination of knowledge, was incompatible with the primal belief that knowledge was sacred power that must be kept only to those deemed worthy of it.

Knowledge was a manifestation of *mana*, the force that energized everything in the universe. *Mana* flowed to men from the original ancestral spirits, and this precious flow was carefully guarded by a system of prohibitions (*kapu*), so that it might reach only those who, by their lineage, talent, or industry could use it to benefit the community. The knowledge of each guild was kept secret to its members—an exclusivity not unlike that practiced by some professional and trade organizations today.

Words transmit knowledge. The spoken word can be restricted to those within hearing distance; but the written word becomes a thing of *mana* that can be stolen by enemies or dissipated among those who may misuse it.

Subsistence vs Market Economies

There was no word for trade or merchant in any Polynesian language. Exchange of goods and services was by a system of reciprocal gift-giving, made intricate by a protocol that recognized differences in status between the parties (to Hawaiians, taxes were gifts that brought honor to the giver, and obligated the ruler to provide justice and security).

Theirs was an affluent subsistence economy with a built-in sense of sufficiency in which exploitation of resources was discontinued when needs were satisfied. When Hawaiians worked, they produced impressively; but when their needs were met, they ceased working—a custom some foreigners regarded as laziness.

These foreigners comprehended only a market economy conducted for profit in which there is no sense of sufficiency. Profits must be re-invested into greater production to create more profits, and markets must be expanded by creating wants as well as satisfying needs. In this spiral of ever-increasing production the exploitation of resources accelerates toward an inevitable scarcity.

THE NEW QUILT *Private Collection*

Voyagers

Voyagers presents a dynamic history filled with images of native kings, star navigators, British explorers—the coming together of vastly different cultures. As Herb Kane's publisher and friend, I have been living and breathing this story for months now in the editing and shaping of Herb's book. It is history I have grown to love.

But many people will be drawn to Voyagers not because it is historical, but because it is historic—the first ART book ever created completely (from type to finished color) on the Macintosh computer. This publication signals the beginning of a whole new way of communicating in print—desktop color without compromise.

BACKGROUND

In October of 1985, our company, Beyond Words Publishing, created two books: *Within a Rainbowed Sea*—a collection of unique underwater images, and *Molokai, An Island in Time*, a photo-autobiography. Produced traditionally on the most expensive Crosfield scanners and optical typesetters, these books won thirty-five national and international awards, including two gold medals at the New York Art Director's Club. Chosen as presidential gifts of state, they were also honored by the Printing Industries of America in 1985 as the "Best Printed Books in America."

Achieving that level of quality resulted in production costs so staggering that to this day the debt has not been repaid, despite record sales.

Worse, was the loss of control. Most of the publishing process was in the hands of a professional elite whose offices and workshops were filled with sophisticated and very expensive proprietary systems for color scanning and image processing. For us, the imperative was clear. To stay in publishing we needed to find a way to reduce our costs, gain back control over the creative process, and lose nothing in final quality.

Our "answer" came with the arrival of the Macintosh Plus and Apple's 300 d.p.i. LaserWriter. Simultaneously a close friend named MacKinnon Simpson called asking for help in creating a three panel color tourist brochure for a tiny whaling museum in Lahaina, Maui.

"Why don't I research and write, and you do the rest, okay?" he asked with a laugh.

Done!

Each of us bought our own Mac Plus, PageMaker Version 1.0, Word 1.05 and set to work. We had 20 megabyte hard drives, a nine inch

screen to scroll around on, one LaserWriter, and a primitive TV scanner from New Image Technologies. Added to that was my burning desire to discover in this nascent technology the answer to our publishing dilema.

We found it indeed! On that little Mac Plus screen we could work miracles of design, changing type on a whim, making pictures bigger or smaller at the nudge of a mouse. MacKinnon got excited and found more pictures and wrote more text. I got excited and made layout after layout. It was so easy. It wasn't long before we saw that our little brochure wanted more than anything to become a book. The client, Rick Ralston gave his consent and in October of 1987, *WhaleSong* was featured on the front page of the New York Times. Hailed as "the most elegant book ever created using a personal computer," *WhaleSong* was the first to use 300 dot per inch LaserWriter type in a coffee-table format. An Australian critic called the story of *WhaleSong's* birth, "the ultimate DTP case history!"

WhaleSong came into a computer world not yet convinced that desktop publishing was good for more than school fliers or an upscale brochure that dared try spot color. *WhaleSong* was proof for many that the dream they had worked on for so long, might soon come true. Apple bought a copy for every dealer in the country, and stories started to appear everywhere in the press..."MONEY" magazine, regional and national newspaper stories, and delightfully, a three page "*PUBLISH!*" editorial.

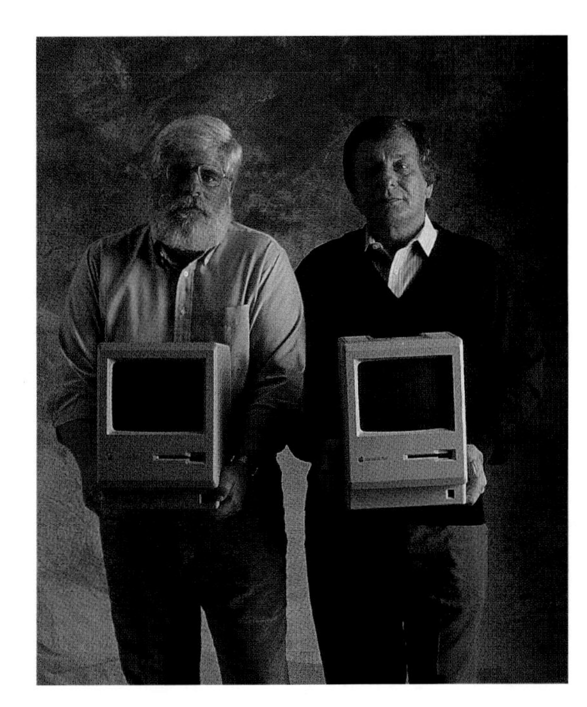

"They said it couldn't be done and they were almost right!"

The first invitations began to arrive for presentations at Seybold, and other industry events, but we were already at work on the next edition of *WhaleSong*. This time we focused on what everyone was confident could NEVER be done on a Mac—high-end continuous tone photographic color reproduction.

We got a little Barneyscan 35mm scanner, a SHARP 300 dpi flatbed scanner, and after much negotiation, an Alpha copy of a new super secret program from Adobe. "This will be the answer to your dreams," said Adobe's Liz Bond, and it was.

The program ended up being called Photoshop, and was from the start bullet-proof. Five minutes after opening the first secret version from Adobe, one of our *WhaleSong* staff looked at the computer screen and said, "that's Barneyscan's XP program!" And it was. Adobe had licensed it from the developers and under the inspired guidance of Adobe's Steve Guttman and Art Director Russell Brown, Photoshop grew to be the industry leader.

Back then, in 1988, Photoshop 1.0 was all that we needed to create amazingly good corrected and separated films on an L-300 imagesetter. *WhaleSong* was entirely re-done, this time in 2400 dpi output, with new pages filled with the first continuous tone color separations. Yes, there was moire patterning. No, it wasn't overwhelmingly visible. Once again, what everyone assumed was impossible turned out to not only be possible, but fairly easy. Invitations came from Sweden, England, Japan, and Australia to come and tell *WhaleSong's* story. These early presentations evolved into the *WhaleSong* Color Seminars—two hour programs that take the viewer from color scanning to imagesetting to the making of overlay printer's proofs.

Intelligent Electronics, Apple's leading reseller, made us their desktop alliance partner and began promoting a series of major city *WhaleSong* Color Seminars. With Apple funding, the most recent was held over three days in Key Biscayne, Florida and was a runaway success. Every presentation was packed.

THE CHALLENGE

The gamble was that the technology we needed...would arrive just in the nick of time.

There was one last peak to climb!

A few people in the world of graphic arts had begun, grudgingly, to admit that quality color just might be possible on a Macintosh desktop platform. But there are few industries more dependent on their high-end equipment than color separation houses. Doctors, perhaps.

Even the few professional color people who ventured that "it might be possible" were quick to add that "parity with the Crosfields and Scitexes of the world was still a long way off, if ever."

Believing their own propaganda, they welcomed things like OPI. To us it seemed that their message was, "Go ahead guys and girls, play with your images on your Macintosh. Fiddle around with Photoshop if you must. But, when you are done playing, just give your files to the PROFESSIONALS, and we will crank out the real stuff—that super high quality perfect film your printer expects from you. Then of course, your bill will reflect our costs for the high-end multi-million dollar equipment we purchased before this desktop thing ever got born." It was an uncomfortable reminder of our horrendously expensive venture into high-end traditional color. I wanted nothing to do with it. Besides, the traditional publishing world had been wrong twice before. *WhaleSong* in both editions was living proof that there just might be another reality out there.

So we committed to doing a new book, and started looking for the right vehicle.

In January of 1991, my old friend, Herb Kane, called to ask my advice on how to get his new book printed in Singapore. My reply surprised us both.

"First of all, I don't think you should print out of the United States, no matter how much you save," I said. "Secondly, we can do it all on the desktop." "Thirdly, by the time you are ready to begin, I'll have my downstairs living room filled with all the equipment we'll need!"

Much to my alarm, Herb immediately agreed to all three points. So, the die was cast!

My intuition that all this was now possible was being put to the ultimate test. Even working in-house, an art book is an expensive undertaking. Our best guess on cost? Over $100,000 before going on press. More like a quarter of a million dollars to see the book into the bookstores nationwide. Where was the desktop technology that would allow us to at least aim at our target?

Many months earlier Lorie and I had visited Howard Barney, inventor of the 35mm scanner that we had used so successfully for our *WhaleSong* books. He had shown us the mock-up of their new multi-format transparency scanner and talked guardedly about the software that would run it.

SHARP had introduced their JX600 flatbed scanner. Photoshop had continued to evolve. PageMaker was out in a new color extension version. And there were rumours of a coming drum scanner product from Agfa that would deliver almost dot perfect screened film everytime.

One of Barney's earliest production models of their new 4520 scanner was the first to arrive. Not long after we added an early version of Agfa's Focus Color scanner.

Herb's hand-drawn thumbnail sketches for the book layout arrived together with over a hundred 4x5 transparencies and we were underway.

I once heard serendipity defined as "the ability to fall into a pile of horse manure and come out smelling like a rose." We had not fallen, as much as willingly jumped, into what easily could have been a disaster. Still, I had good reason to expect success. At an ever increasing rate, I had seen the computer industry find color publishing solutions. The gamble was that the technology to create our art book would arrive just in the nick of time. And that's the way it happened.

On June 30th, Agfa's SelectSet 5000 arrived at our doorstep. Barney's newest version of Color Access software was hand-carried to us from Australia where it was in continuous development.

BETTER THAN WE DARED HOPE!

At the heart of our entire publishing effort lies a remarkable scanner with its accompanying software...

Most amazing of all was that we became only the *second* U.S. Beta site for testing Agfa's Balanced Screening Technology. This was technology so new that there was no rational reason to expect it to work as advertised. But it did. We downloaded the 175 line screen round-dot software into our Emerald RIP and then began making separations around-the-clock.

Everything came together to allow Herb's book to become the first of its kind in the world.

Ladies and Gentlemen...get out your loupes!

Sexy Hardware And Software

One corner of our production area houses the 4520 Barneyscanner pictured at right. It has been sitting there, turned on day and night, for almost six months. During the past 45 days we have used it to scan hundreds of transparencies, from 35mm to 4x5s, with a success ratio that would stretch the credulity of a true believer. Try 90%. Some days we hit 95%. Every once in a while we finish a run of Cromacheck proofs only to discover that every single one is top quality. No redos. There is, of course, reason behind all this.

Part of the reason centers on the pixie-like genius and charm of inventor Howard Barney. Everything in his machine works as designed. The other key ingredient is Barneyscan's Australian team, one a computer and publishing wizard named John Stewart, the other a master printer and teacher named David Alexander.

Bob Goodman with the Barneyscan 4520 and "friends."

The software they created, called QuickScan and ColorAccess, is focused on solving real world color production problems. David Alexander knew these all too well from his job as head of Sydney Technical University's prepress department. David graduates 1,200 students a year from a three-year curriculum that implements the finest traditional color scanning and printing technology in the world. In true Australian fashion, John Stewart and David Alexander battled for years to create software that would allow an unsophisicated end-user to obtain quality scans using default settings. Before we took delivery of our 4520, I was told by John Stewart that 85 to 90 percent of all the transparencies we needed to scan could be successfully imaged this way. In other words, the overwhelming power of the software—equaling or surpassing high-end systems—is available as the operator's skill levels increase. At its most sophisticated, the interface remains kindly. The learning curve stays gentle.

Stewart and Alexander understood that if you set your tonal values correctly, the color will largely take care of itself. QuickScan sets its tonal values by asking you to prescan, then to select a highlight point plus a shadow point, and then finally to scan. A powerful 386 computer in the 4520 does the rest. These four steps take only a few minutes and can be learned by anyone in less than an hour.

Two other production issues have been solved in the software. First, a job setting file is created for every scan and is linked to the original scan each time separations are called for. Expert users can create job parameters once so that they can be used repeatedly by less skilled operators.The result is high repeatability and speed in creating new scans as well as in handling client changes. The original RGB scan remains unaltered.

The second production issue is achieving full use of your scanning workstation. Separation routines can be lengthy. The 4520 with Color Access works in the background, freeing your computer and your operator for other productive jobs.

HIGH END DESKTOP COLOR—

For many companies, the $260,000 system below can pay for itself in 6 to 18 months.

Our goal in creating *Voyagers* was to test a new desktop publishing package that made full use of the emerging color technology. This time, using the newest Agfa screening technology, we decided to aim for "showcase" color.

In *WhaleSong's* first two editions, we had learned how to maximize the results from our original equipment choices, most of which stayed the same for the new *Voyagers* book. The most significant change was moving from the Linotronic L-300 to Agfa's new SelectSet 5000.

Other new additions to our pick of the best available desktop color technology are incorporated in our final system pictured at right. Everything shown was tested except for the late arriving Tektronix Phaser III color printer. Because the QuickSCSI and Radius Rocket were in pre-release versions, we did not want to risk our working system with possible incompatibility problems. So we created an isolated system to confirm their performance and waited for production models to be included as pictured here.

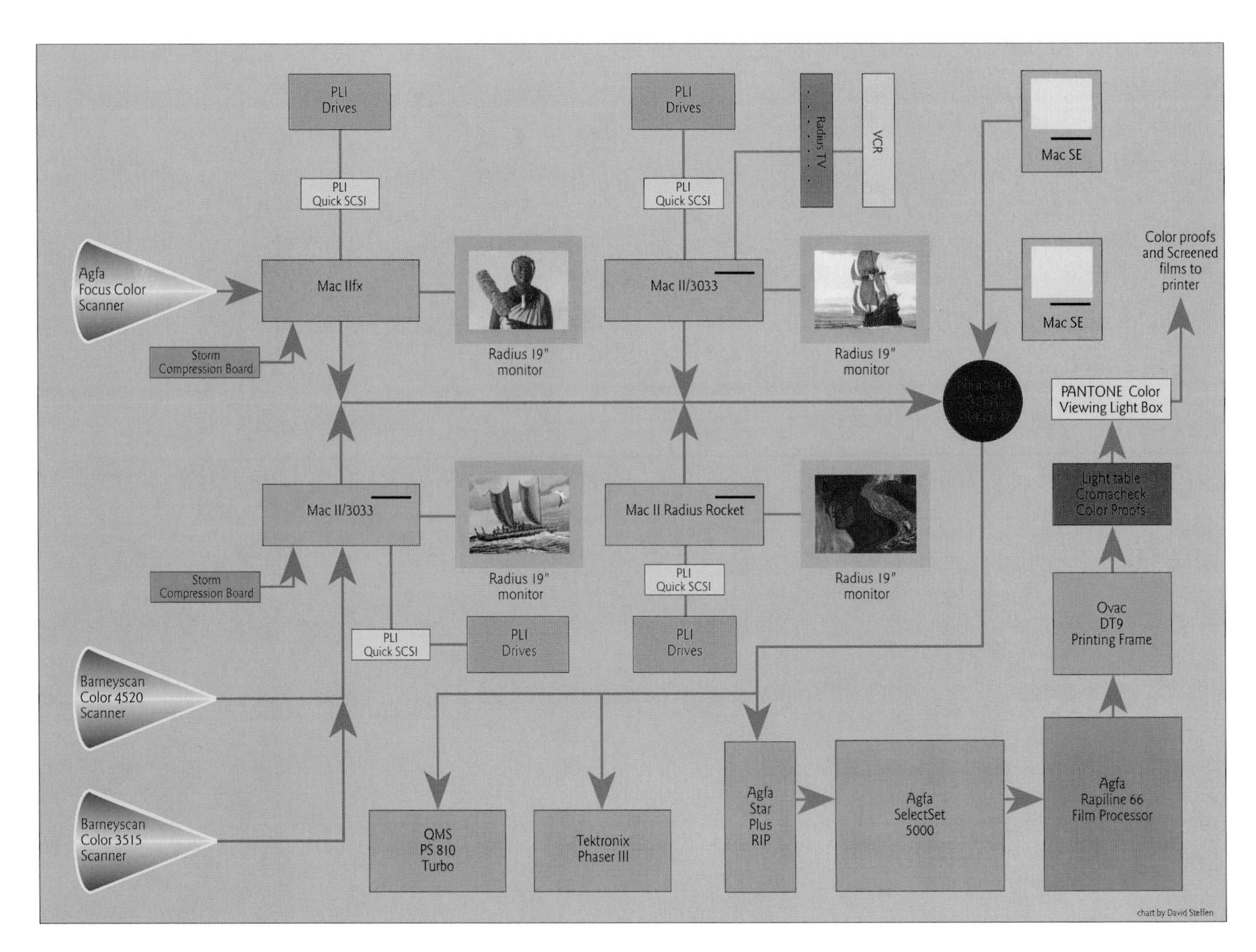

BASIC HARDWARE

Here is what works for us, based on five years of experimenting to find the best tools.

My first hard drive ever was a LoDown 20 meg device that I bought in early 1986. My choice was between Apple's 20 meg drive—slow as a slug but nearly bullet-proof—and the LoDown, which was creating a stir because it was selling for under a thousand dollars. I bought one figuring that with a name like that it had to be good. I was lucky. The people behind LoDown cared about their customers. The drive lasted uncommonly long. And, my deep seated belief to pay as much attention to the people behind the product, as to the whiz-bang technical specifications (or price) was once again validated.

Having said that, I'd like to share my thoughts about the equipment needed for high-end color on the desktop.

The Computer

Showcase quality color demands as much power as you can afford. We have four Mac IIs of various lineages. Two have Siclone 3033 accelerators, one is an fx, the fourth has the Radius Rocket on board. It is blazingly fast, and in the right configuration, a major boost to productivity.

Our Mac IIfx is a solid performer. As to the soon- to-be-released Tower and desktop 040 models? I can't wait to build an even more powerful workstation around them.

Storing Data and Moving it Around

Our experiences with PLI, both their products and as a company, have been exemplary. Innovative and dedicated to delivering quality, their entire line of Turbo drives works *together*. We routinely mix magneto opticals, 45 meg removables, 300 and 600 meg Turbo drives. Having everything from one manufacturer is a plus. The PLI QuickSCSI card gives us a very fast second SCSI chain. It saves both time and money by speeding transfers of data significantly.

Memory

Our Radius 040 Rocket rushed us into the world of four megabyte simms, but it took MAXIMA, a memory extension utility from Connectix, to get us into the 14 meg and above RAM disks, a world of instantaneous response. It is addictive and a super BIG time saver.

Power Conditioning

Hawaii is blessed with many things, but one of them isn't clean, surge free electricity. As a result, we live by the protection we get from the big Kensington Power Backer UPS units, backed up by MasterPiece units for each of our Macs. Another case of a company that cares about their customers.

Printers, Black and White, and Color

For black and white laser printers, QMS is our choice, hands down. In a crowded field, they are the leaders. Being a graphic production house, our laser printers can go through a toner cartridge a day, and these QMS printers are workhorses.

For color comping, our choice, again hands down, is the new Phaser III from Tektronix. If you are serious about production color, you must have 11x17 inch bleed capability in your comping device, plain paper output, 300 dpi resolution, PostScript Level 2 software, accelerated RISC based processor, two sided printing and CIE calibrated colors. The Phaser III has it all. From what we can see, this is THE break-through product for the desktop color world. The neatest touch of all is that you can load the ink blindfolded in a dark room. Hey you! No peeking!

Monitors

Radius remains our favorite. Why? My heart says that if I am going to be camped in front of a monitor day in and day out, I deserve the *best* the industry can offer. My head says that Radius engineering is simply superior. For instance, the Radius Precision Color Calibrator gives me enough predictability to do color correction based on the monitor image alone. That's not how I am *supposed* to do it, but that's how I *actually* do it, quite often.

You can create a professional color proof in your office for $5 worth of material and ten minutes worth of time!

Cromacheck Color Proofing

The best hardware we know for "contract proofing" is the OVAC-24, an ultra-violet vacuum printing frame made by OLEC in Irvine, CA.

Exposing Du Pont Cromacheck film in the OVAC gives us high quality overlay color proofs from our separations for around $5 each. We place our imagesetter films on the appropriate color of Cromacheck and expose in the printing frame for a few seconds. Fully developed by the UV light, a simple pull strips off the top layer of each of the four colors. Combined in register, these four layers become our color proof. No darkroom. No chemicals. Almost no skill. Cromacheck proofs are a fine entry level desktop proofing system.

On balance, Cromacheck leads the world today for both ease of use, environmental *and* pocketbook friendliness. That's quite a distinction!

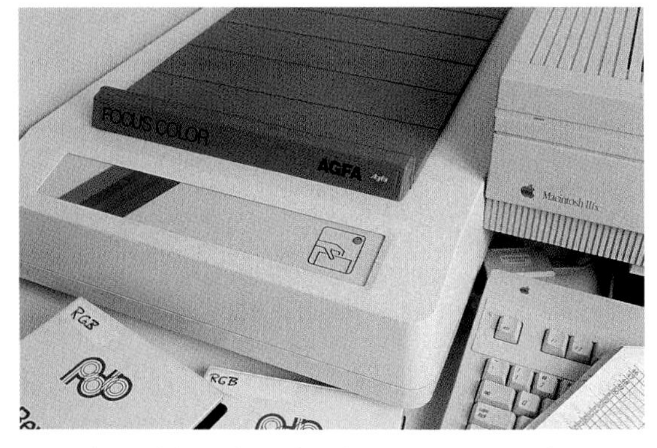

Our early model 800 dpi Agfa color scanner. A SCSI device, the new Focus Color Plus handles transparencies as well.

Network Connections

We've experimented with software solutions like Timbuktu and Data Club. Too slow, too cumbersome. PhoneNet connectors work well with LocalTalk, but choke on the data load. So we installed the industry leading Asanté Ethernet boards to pump data to our SelectSet RIP. They work like a charm! Our next step is to find a headless dedicated file server.

Wrist Resters

A product called, TrackPad or WristPad comes from a company called Silicon Sports. Until Tony Hodges gets his ergonometric keyboard to market, little helpers like these colorful pads, or the best-selling LifeGuard program from Visionary Software will help protect you from debilitating stress injuries like carpal tunnel syndrome.

One of our four 19 inch Radius Monitors. The scanned image is being displayed in Barneyscan's Color Access program which allows accurate CMYK readouts and very precise prepress color controls. The images in this book speak volumes about the built-in intelligence in this color correction and separation program.

HARDWARE AND SOFTWARE

From the first moment I opened PageMaker 1.0, I felt empowered, and the feeling has never gone away.

SPEAKING TO MY MACINTOSH

When I was a little kid and home alone, I would talk to just about anything. Why Not? To me everything was alive... telephone poles, my toy soldiers, my Dad's car, and my sled. My life extended everywhere! In 1985, when I was introduced to the Macintosh Plus computer my life changed. Did I have feelings for this machine? Did I talk to it when people were not looking? Sure! The kid in me, happily enough, was still alive and well.

Now along comes a product from Articulate Systems called Voice Navigator that lets me *really* talk to my Mac. Communicate with it. Command it to do things. And it does! All I have to do is say just about any command on the menu and my Mac will execute it to perfection. At last my Mac has become a hard working Beta version of an Android. Wow!

PAGE LAYOUT

The DTP world seems divided into those who love and use PageMaker and those who use Quark Xpress. Everyone I know has both. People tell me constantly that PageMaker is behind Xpress in the features war, and in a few areas, that is true. But PageMaker has something very special going for it— Paul Brainerd's dream of opening the page layout world to everyone. Aldus has never waivered from that goal—the greatest good for the

PageMaker layout for Voyagers. Yellow highlighted text shows us lines that do not conform fully to our programmed instructions.

multitude. In fairness, Quark has never waivered from their goal of serving professional Macintosh users. To each his own.

If I absolutely positively must have a few special features, I open Xpress and use them. But for day-in and day-out work, for the creative stuff, PageMaker makes me feel good. Besides, software companies play leap-frog routinely and Aldus is no slouch as a competitor. Their day will come again.

PageMaker with PrePrint 1.5 (see the illustration below) now supports the DCS file format. The steps are simple and straightforward.

I can't think of a better entry level package than PageMaker/PrePrint for people just getting their feet wet in color prepress.

IMAGE CREATION AND MANIPULATION

There are three staple programs: Aldus FreeHand (see the color illustrations in this section), Illustrator from Adobe, and the third, a program that combines both creative tools and highly developed prepress image manipulation abilities—Adobe's Photoshop.

In its newest incarnation, version 2.0, Photoshop delivers a host of expanded features. For color matching systems you can now choose between Pantone, Trumatch, or Focoltone. Display CMYK bitmaps? Duotone generation? Video input or output? All these and more are part of this history-making program that, for us, made the creation of *WhaleSong,* and now *Voyagers,* fun.

HEADLINE HAPPINESS

Not used in this book, but worth including in every library is TypeStyler from Brøderbund.

THE END GAME/PART ONE

Ultimately the editorial process is reduced to trillions of perfectly modulated and placed specs of light—imagesetting.

Laying Down The Dots

Voyagers could not have happened if a young engineer at Agfa had not dedicated a good chunk of his professional life to creating a new imagesetter called the SelectSet 5000.

One of the highlights of my six years in the world of computers was meeting that young man, Brian Rooney, at Agfa's headquarters.

Lorie and I were there to see with our own eyes what so many people were saying was a superb new machine, and it was Brian Rooney who met us with a big smile. Without a wasted motion he asked if we would like to see the imagesetters in the process of assembly.

I remember walking around for more than an hour, looking and asking questions, my tape recorder on while Brian told us every detail and more about his creation.

We were delighted to hear that the SelectSet was as American as apple pie—conceived, engineered, and assembled in the U.S. He explained the very heavy cast and machined frame that was necessary to maintain the extreme precision required of every unit. He showed us the drum assembly that would hold the film stationary during exposure and explained why it was only 170 degrees of a circle. The reason? So that light going down during exposure could not reflect upwards and have a direct reflected path back to degrade the image.

There were dozens of these small engineering triumphs. One was as simple as four small plastic cups to catch the film punched automatically if registration holes were requested by the operator. Another was the use of a super high speed motor to spin the mirror that distributes the laser imaging beam. And the mirror, unlike other laser imaging devices was only a single surface.

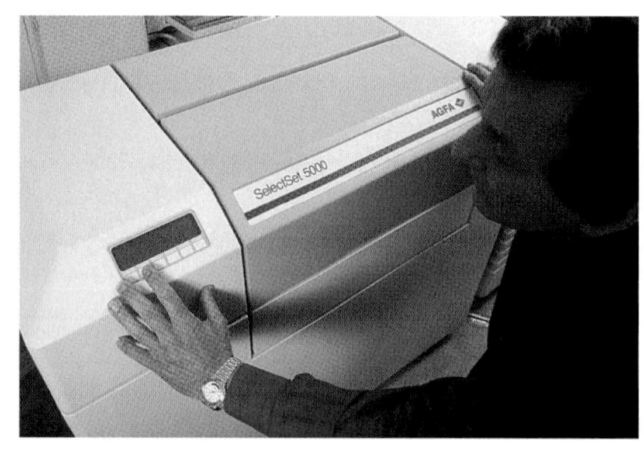

Our imagesetter at home in Hawaii. We gave it its very own power circuit, clean cool dry air, and our Aloha.

The control panel was itself a marvel of built-in intelligence, an LCD visual feast of almost obvious icons that offered you a sense of safety in operating the machine. A 3600 dpi option would soon be announced to be followed by a still larger model imagesetter.

I came away awed by the design and engineering excellence I saw at every turn. In fairness, I am not an engineer. But I have done major high technology essays covering everything from rocketry to space satellites. I knew I had just seen a winner in the imagesetter derby. How it would actually perform, I would soon discover.

Seven weeks later four very large perspiring moving men lifted the over six hundred pound imagesetter off its shipping base and carried it effortlessly into the downstairs of our studio in Honolulu. An Agfa service man, resident in Hawaii, was on our doorstep the next morning to get us up and running. Ten rolls of 16 inch daylight loading ZHN Zebra film were stacked and ready. Our new processor arrived in a few days later and was assembled in just hours. No plumbing.

Switches were thrown. The RIP blinked ready. And either the second or third image was a fine set of separations. This is a very boring story. It gets worse. We've been running the SelectSet 18 hours a day for the last 60 days. Hundreds and hundreds of pages have been generated with not a single jam or misfeed, or problem of any kind.

My personal workstation. A transparency viewing box is on the left, and my black VCR is ready to hook up to Radius TV.

PART TWO/SCREEN PATTERNS

Moire patterns are mathematically impossible with Balanced ScreenTechnology!

What about calibration? We bought Precision and have never used it. Checked three times a day, our D-Max ranges from 3.9 to 4.1. Our percentage bars are never more than 2% off, generally within 1% or dead on. It is easily the least exciting machine I have ever owned—except for what it does—witness this book. To us that's beyond exciting. We are speechless!

PERFORMANCE FIGURES

Our SelectSet generates full pages of text in two to three minutes. Pages with text and continuous tone reproductions process in 20 minutes or less average. Full page pictures run in approximately 13 minutes. In creating this book the RIP was consistently faster than us.

A few months after meeting Brian Rooney, Lorie and I were back in Boston, this time on a quest to get a Beta version of the yet to be announced Balanced Screen Technology. All that we had heard suggested that it would at least be the equal of Adobe's Accurate Screens or Linotype's new technology. Little did we expect that we would have a chance to meet the man whose basic research made this new Agfa screen technology possible. After dinner one evening, he drove us back to our hotel and shared these thoughts with us during the drive. Tall, charmingly European, and thin, his name is Paul Delabastita. These are his words...

WHERE OR HOW DID YOU FIRST BECOME AWARE OF THE SCREEN ANGLE PROBLEM? WHY WERE YOU WORKING IN THIS AREA TO BEGIN WITH.

Actually I started working on this subject as part of a project that is completely buried by now by Agfa, a project called Mosaic. The concept of the project was very advanced for 1986. At that time we had the 9600 which could only run at 1200 dpi. So I was given the task of coming up with a set of working screen algorithms which could be used at 1200 dpi with a 9600 imagesetter. This was for color images. So the screens that had to be developed needed to meet all the standards for high quality color reproduction. They had to be moire free, they had to be able to reproduce a complete range of tonality.

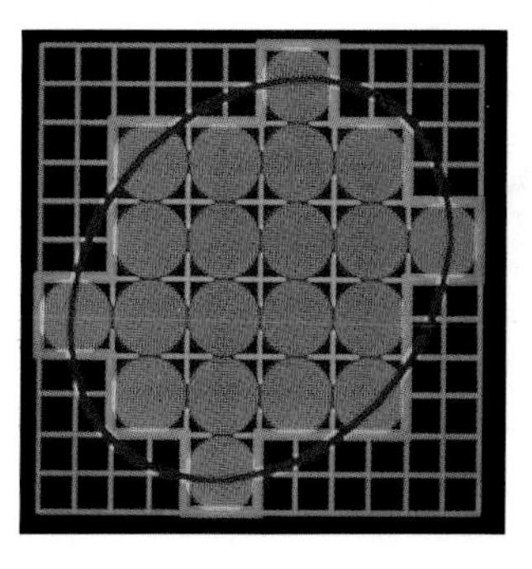

THIS WAS LONG BEFORE IT WAS POSSIBLE TO CREATE ACCURATE ANGLES IN POSTSCRIPT?

This was long before Postscript was even known or accepted as a standard in the industry. Because if PostScript would have existed as a standard we would have never started developing this project. But the basic problems were the same, moire free reproduction of color images. I started by actually making a careful mathematical analysis why the conventional system for color reproductionworks. What is the exact reason that you get such good results from the 15/45/75 system?

WHAT IS THE REASON? I'VE LIVED IN COLOR ALL MY LIFE AND I DON'T KNOW WHY.

The reason is a mathematical reason. The moire that is caused by the first set of two screens causes a

It really was a discovery, not an invention. It was wonderful, almost as if it were designed by somebody to work this way!

second order of moire with the third screen that has an infinite period. So if you have the 15 and the 45 degree screens with exactly the same ruling and you overlay them, a very fine moire occurs which is by itself usually invisible and certainly not disturbing. Now if you overlay the third screen, this 75 degree screen causes interference with the moire caused by the first two, and that moire has an infinite period which means that you don't see it, it falls off the page completely. And having understood that mathematical relationship which guarantees absolutely moire free color reproduction, that was the key to understanding how to do the same thing again.

HOW WOULD YOU DESCRIBE BALANCED SCREENING TECHNOLOGY?

It stands for a screening system where the three angles and rulings for the cyan, magenta, and black are mathematically adjusted to each other to cancel out moire completely and to obtain infinitely large moire periods. In addition, BST also increases the frequency of the yellow raster to solve some well known problems from the yellow printer.

DOES THIS WORK ACROSS ALL THE FREQUENCIES?

Yes. From 1,200 dpi to 3600 dpi and from 65 line screen to 300 line screen.

SO, I STILL HAVE A QUESTION ABOUT THE HELL HQS APPROACH AND AGFA'S SCREENING TECHNOLOGY.

There is a fundamental difference between the HQS approach (which replicates a tile under an angle) and having tiles with pre-angled dots replicated horizontally and vertically. You can obtain exactly the same angles with both methods, yet in one case you will find that you always end up with some left over moire like HQS. It might be a very long moire, but it simply doesn't cancel out completely.The way we do it, however, just cancels it out completely, almost in a wonderful fashion as if it were designed by somebody to work this way. And I discovered it...it was a long difficult process to discover it, but I would really like to describe it as a discovery rather than as an invention or even the result of an analytical process.

DO YOU REMEMBER THE MOMENT YOU ACTUALLY HAD THE INSIGHT INTO THE SOLUTION?

Yes, I was at home in my apartment studying the problem very intensely and trying to understand the relationships between the frequencies of screens. And then suddenly by drawing a square frame around a triangle I suddenly saw the answer and realized that the problem was resolved.

WHAT WAS IT THAT YOU SAW?

That I had found a way to cancel out moire completely and to make the moire period infinitely large.

ONCE YOU HAD THAT INSIGHT, WHAT STEPS DID YOU TAKE SO THAT A SET OF FILTERS OR SCREEN ANGLES COULD BE CREATED?

Well, for a very long time no work at all was done on this technology. For many years it was just that we knew it works and was available. We were very aware, also, of the limitations of PostScript. So it was not until recently, late 1989 and early 1990 when PostScript became more functional, that we could put our discovery into effect.

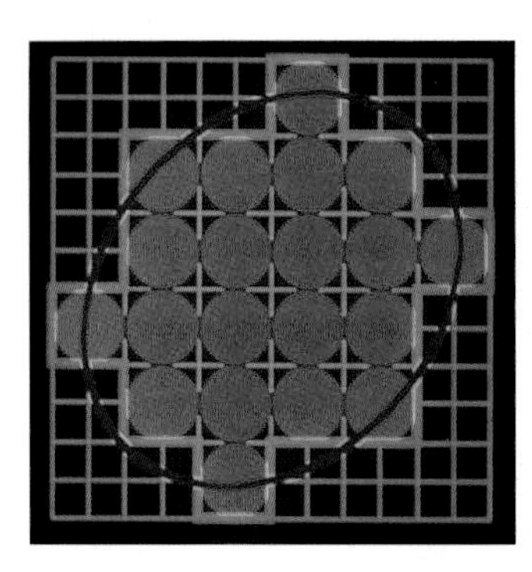

COMPRESSION & CALIBRATION

The Agony and the Ecstasy

As a desktop publisher I am drowning in data. I have 20 optical disks now, 80 SyQuests, perhaps three hundred floppies, all full. In desperation I turned first to Radius ImpressIt software which does a great job on smaller files. Then needing more horsepower and charmed by the 60 MIPS of processing power claim, I got the PicturePress Accelerator card from Storm Technology.

What I really got, for the first time ever, was some compression information that makes sense to the photographer in me.

Image quality? The amount of compression is directly related to image quality . But the complexity of the image (the amount of redundant visual info) and the amount of information you need to compress are also factors. One way to insure image quality is to scan the image at higher dpi settings than normal. This gives greater pixel density. The more pixels you have the more you can compress without seeing the diference. You have more quality and a smaller file if you scan high and compress, than if you scan at a lower dpi initially.

I've learned to use compression where it makes sense and leave it out where it doesn't. Compress at ratios of 8:1 and you will see no difference, or compress at 40:1 and gain the speed for displaying and moving files. You can use compression in your final images or just in your placement proofs. The entire process is a compromise. You can compromise a lot, or a little, or not at all. It depends on how much time/money you want to trade off.

Meeting deadlines is what prepress production is all about. How fast can you display, view, move, or transmit images is directly dependent on the size of the image. The larger the image the longer it takes. With compression you can decrease your time to do these tasks directly by the compression level you choose. So with a 20:1 compression level you can now transmit and move that file 20 times faster—nine minutes instead of three hours.

The PicturePress accelerator card works as advertised, so fast that you are seldom aware of any delay in closing or opening files. Impressive! Used intelligently, it is a clear moneymaker.

Bob Goodman and Production Chief, Ken Kimura use a color temperature controlled viewing box to evaluate Cromacheck proofs, matching them to Focoltone swatches.

The Business Of Calibration

"It helps when everyone speaks a common language." In the graphic arts world, the Herbert family was first out of the blocks in seeing a need to standardize colors for the printers and their customers. PANTONE was born and established itself as a world standard, the leader. And then, as desktop technology began to open the door to a flood of color printing, it became clear that PANTONE simply didn't work like it needed to in the world of CMYK, the four process colors all printers use.

Enter the charming story of a Master Printer in Cardiff, Wales named Gordon Phillips, who simply could not stand to have clients hovering over his presses and demanding more cyan here and less magenta there. Correcting color on the press is foolhardy and expensive and not veryeffective.The solution came one day when talking to an advertising agency art director, Gordon picked up a swatch of each of the four process colors and said, "Do you have any idea how many colors are hidden in these four CMYK inks?

"How many?" asked the art director.

"I don't know," answered Gordon honestly, "but I'll find out and let you know." The number he came back with was 763, and the way he arrived at that number has become the FOCOLTONE—short for four color tone—system. Crosfield incorporated it in their high end system immediately. It is one of those wonderfully intuitive discoveries that happen from time to time.

CALIBRATION

The FOCOLTONE colors are created by removing screens from each CMYK family of four. These family colors are the only ones in the FOCOLTONE system which need four screens to produce a color. Taking one color screen away at a time produces four new colors (three screens for each color). Taking away two at a time produces six more colors (two screens for each color). Taking away three screens leaves the four single colors (one screen for each color).

In all an astonishing 46 colors can be produced from the original four screens of each line, and there are 15 such available palettes.

Many color applications call for spot color printing and not process color. Many applications require colors to be reproduced both ways. Because all FOCOLTONE colors have been converted to single mix spot colors using only the four CMYK inks, it is possible to work in CMYK on a color monitor and specify where required, the spot mix to the printer.

Gordon Phillips saw that his system could produce process colors to a known reference standard. He also knew that the dot structure of these colors when they were being printed would obey the same rules as the changes in the dot structure of the more complicated separation sets.

Include a FOCOLTONE color on the printers form and if the FOCOLTONE COLOR looks right, the separations are being correctly printed. This is the first time the printer has had an adequate objective reference to the quality of his printing.

THE ELEGANCE OF TYPE

He was thirty when he drew an alphabet, forty-six before he counted himself a professional type designer. Yet by the end of his long life Frederic Goudy had become the most famous type designer in the world. This eccentric American created more than a hundred faces, including perhaps a dozen that rank among the best ever made. He was an exasperating loner, but he used his celebrity to stimulate and enliven debates about type and typography that amounted to a kind of national education in the aesthetics of type design.

from Masters of American Design
by D.J.R Bruckner

Eric Hornaday, a type production artist, is digitizing from an original Lanston Monotype drawing using IKARUS-M onthe Macintosh.

This introduction to Frederic Goudy is relevant here because of a unique chain of circumstances that led to *Voyagers* becoming the first book in 40 to 50 years to be set in Goudy Village No. 2.

The story begins with the arrival in Honolulu (enroute to Los Angeles) of an Australian type master named Paul Soady. A mutual friend had introduced us to each other by phone and something about the way it all happened told me to meet this person. It was a delight! Witty, conservative, wonderfully human, in two hours of non-stop conversation Paul Soady literally transported me into the magic world of type. I asked, and he promised to help with this book, and so not many weeks later I phoned him to ask about possible typefaces. He told me that digital type was a horrid development but that if I insisted on using it there was one company whose type was quite good, the Font Company in Scottsdale, Arizona. They had, Paul continued, a truly lovely face called Goudy Village No. 2. Would I consider it for our book?

It took me all of five minutes to pick up the phone and within days we had the face you are reading now, digitized directly from the 1932 drawings of Goudy's design. It is everything and more that I believed PostScript-based type could be. Further, The Font Company was willing to slightly modify the typeface to include macron accents which might be necessary for certain Hawaiian words. This is the first and only time that the original character set of a Lanston typeface has been changed by The Font Company.

By the end of his long life, Frederic Goudy had become the most famous type designer in the world.

At my request they sent me copious background information on this typeface and on Goudy himself. One piece of that background information is worth reprinting here in its entirety.

"In 1903, as proprietor of the Village Press, Frederic W. Goudy designed and cut a bookface for use as his house face. This design, his first complete bookface was named Village. In 1932, while art director of The Lanston Monotype Co., Philadel-phia, he revised the original design. The result was Goudy Village No. 2. On the original specimen sheet, notes state "In this letter Goudy has not sought to duplicate his first attempt at letter cutting, but out of the ripeness of his experience and developed taste, he has redrawn the Village type as he would have it today. A comparison of this letter with the original design, cut by Goudy thirty-five years ago, is evidence of the improvement which has intervened between the first Village Type and this more recent design. The modification and the refinement are the fruit of Mr. Goudy's matured artistry."

It is well-known that much of Goudy's lifework was lost when his workshop was burned to the ground on January 26th, 1939. What is not com-mon knowledge is that a body of Goudy's work, original drawings and pencil tracings, was safe in the Laston offices. There they remained until a day in the 1960s. On this day Lanston management de-cided that pencil-on-bristol drawings were unnecessary because metal patterns existed. The drawings were carried out and thrown into the trash. A passerby asked to be given the drawings, complete for more than 200 Lanston faces including work by both Goudy and Sol Hess. The company agreed. For more than 25 years, these drawings were hidden away, their existence unknown to most of the world. Now, The Font Company, Inc. has secured exclusive access to the entire collection, prior to it presentation to The Smithsonian Institution as a national treasure. The Font Company is pleased to announce as its first PostScript language release in this historic restoration project, Goudy Village No.2."

An original Lanston drawing, pencil-on-bristol.

A BRIEF NOTE ABOUT THE RESTORATION PROJECT

The entire 275+ face master drawing collection is now in Arizona. Digitization begins with the sorting of drawings for a particular font. The complete character sets are assembled and decisions made on the best point size on which to model the PostScript version. Organizing the drawings is not always an easy task as the draw-ings may include many alternate characters, differences in ascenders and descenders, and even some characters drawn but never cut.

A sheet of tracing paper is placed over each drawing. A type production artist lightly marks each line end-ing, corner point and curve tangent, based on an invisible grid of 15,000 by 15,000 units per em-square. Using a cross-hair puck and a digitizing tablet, the artist manually captures each point into the IKARUS system. For any one complete typeface, this can involve 5,000 points or more. The original baselines and sidebearings noted on the drawing are used. Each character is fully inspected for fidelity to the drawing.

This unique type restoration project has been dedicated to the Marder family. Thanks to Dick Marder, the Lanston Monotype Type Library is being preserved—as useful fonts available to communicators in digital format and as a typographic art treasure for future generations.

Warmest Mahalo to to our friends for their Kokua:

David Alexander
Diane Anderson
Tom Barosky
Belknap Imaging—
Buzz Belknap
Mike Garrity
Matt Heim
Kym Miller
Scott Matsushige
Scott and Maria Tome
Stephen Kapali.
Paul Berry
Peter Broderick
Paul Buxbaum
Larry Cooke
Paul Delabastita
Fred Dempsey
Michael Falcon
Peter Fink
Steve Hayward
Gene Hunt
Ken Kimura
Char and Byron Liske
Tim Lynch
Tom Moore
Bill and Anna O'Brien
Al Perelli
Abo Peterson
Lou Prestia
Brian Rooney
Joe Schuld
MacKinnon Simpson
Al Sisto
Joe Solem
David Steffen
John Stewart
Chuck Surprise
Carol Vitagliano
Walter Wright
Mary Woollen

For information regarding the tools and technology used in the making of this book— please contact:

Adobe Systems, Inc. 800-344-8335
Agfa Compugraphic Division 800-227-2780
Aldus Corp. 800-332-5387
Apple Computer, Inc. 408-996-1010
Articulate Systems 617-876-5236
Asanté Technologies, Inc. 408-752-8350
Barneyscan Corp. 415-521-3388
Brøderbund Software 800-521-6263
Colby Systems 415-941-9090
Connectix Corp. 800-950-5880
DuPont 800-654-4567 Ext. 702
Dynagraphics Printing 800-325-8732
Farallon Computing, Inc. 415-849-2331
Focoltone 913-338-0505
The Font Company 800-443-FONT
Kensington Microware 800-535-4242
OLEC Corp. 800-874-6532
Pantone, Inc. 800-222-1149
PLI - Peripheral Land 800-288-8754
QMS, Inc. 800-858-1597
Radius, Inc. 800-227-2795
Sharp Electronics Corp. 800-526-0264
Software Architects 206-487-0122
Storm Technology 415-691-1111
SyQuest Technology 415-490-7511
S.D. Warren Paper Company 617-423-7300
Tektronix, Inc. 800-458-4196
Visionary Software, Inc. 503-246-6200

For additional copies of this book please call Toll Free 800-Whale-89.